W0105952

ENGLISH
FOR EVERYONE
JUNIOR

BEGINNER'S COURSE

PRACTICE BOOK

FREE AUDIO
website and app

www.dkefe.com/junior/uk

Author

Ben Ffrancon Davies is a freelance writer and translator. He writes textbooks and study guides on a wide range of subjects including ELT, history, and literature. He also works on general non-fiction books for children and adults. Ben studied Medieval and Modern Languages at the University of Oxford, and has taught English in France and Spain.

Course consultant

Susannah Reed is an experienced author and educational consultant, specializing in Primary ELT materials. She has taught in Spain and the UK and has worked in educational publishing for over 20 years, as both a publisher and a writer of ELT course books for children around the world.

Language consultant

Professor Susan Barduhn is an English-language teacher, teacher trainer, and author, who has contributed to numerous publications. She has been President of the International Association of Teachers of English as a Foreign Language, and an adviser to the British Council and the US State Department. She is currently a professor at the School of International Training in Vermont.

ENGLISH
FOR EVERYONE
JUNIOR
BEGINNER'S COURSE
PRACTICE BOOK

FREE AUDIO
website and app

www.dkefe.com/junior/uk

Senior Editor Ben Ffrancon Davies
Senior Art Editor Amy Child
Illustrators Amy Child, Dan Crisp
Managing Editor Carine Tracanelli
Managing Art Editor Anna Hall
Senior Production Editor Andy Hilliard
Production Editor Gillian Reid
Senior Production Controllers Samantha Cross, Jude Crozier
Jacket Design Development Manager Sophia MTT
Senior Jacket Designer Surabhi Wadhwa-Gandhi
Jacket Designer Juhi Sheth
Senior Jackets Coordinator Priyanka Sharma-Saddi
DTP Designer Rakesh Kumar
Publisher Andrew Macintyre
Associate Publishing Director Liz Wheeler
Art Director Karen Self
Publishing Director Jonathan Metcalf

First published in Great Britain in 2022 by
Dorling Kindersley Limited
DK, 20 Vauxhall Bridge Road, London SW1V 2SA

The authorised representative in the EEA is
Dorling Kindersley Verlag GmbH. Arnulfstr. 124,
80636 Munich, Germany

Copyright © 2022 Dorling Kindersley Limited
A Penguin Random House Company
10 9 8 7 6 5
006–322065–Mar/2022

All rights reserved.
No part of this publication may be reproduced, stored in or introduced into a retrieval system, or transmitted, in any form, or by any means (electronic, mechanical, photocopying, recording, or otherwise), without the prior written permission of the copyright owner.

A CIP catalogue record for this book
is available from the British Library.
ISBN: 978-0-2414-7113-5

Printed and bound in China

www.dk.com

MIX
Paper | Supporting
responsible forestry
FSC™ C018179

This book was made with Forest Stewardship Council™ certified paper – one small step in DK's commitment to a sustainable future. Learn more at
www.dk.com/uk/information/sustainability

Contents

About the course   6

1 My friends   10

2 At school   16

3 Our classroom   24

4 My things   30

5 Our favourite animals   38

6 This is my family   46

7 This is my room   54

8 Review: This is me   62

9 At the fair   64

10 Our pets   72

11 My body   80

12 Our town   88

13 My home   96

14 Review: Where I live   104

15 On the farm   106

16 Sports   114

17 At the food market   124

18 At the toyshop   132

19 Our hobbies   140

20 Review: What I like   148

21 Our party clothes   150

22 Our day on the beach   158

23 Lunch time   166

24 At the park   174

25 My day   182

26 Review: Me and my day   192

Handwriting guide   194

Answers   199

Acknowledgments   224

About the course

English for Everyone Junior: Beginner's Practice Book is a companion to the *English for Everyone Junior: Beginner's Course*. The course book is divided into 26 units – each with its own theme – and the practice book mirrors that structure. There is audio for all the units.

Our characters

A group of six friends – Maria, Sofia, Ben, Andy, Sara, and Max – help you practise language in a natural and friendly way.

Unit structure

Each practice unit starts with a scene that presents the vocabulary taught in the corresponding course book unit. The child then practises this vocabulary along with the grammar rules they learned in that unit of the course book.

1 New vocabulary

The illustrated scene helps the child practise the vocabulary, as they listen to each word and write it in the correct space.

2 Vocabulary practice

There is more vocabulary practice. The child might be asked to match vocabulary to pictures or spell individual words.

3 Grammar practice

Each unit then practises the grammar rules taught in the corresponding course book unit while also revising vocabulary.

4 Grammar practice

More grammar is practised. Many units also have a song to help learn new grammar and vocabulary.

Audio

English for Everyone Junior: Beginner's Practice Book features extensive supporting audio resources. Listening to and repeating the audio recordings will help the child to master the pronunciation and stress patterns of English, as well as help them to fix new language in their memory.

Register at **www.dkefe.com/junior/uk** to access the audio materials for free. Each file can be played, paused, and repeated as often as you like.

 All vocabulary scenes, songs, and listening exercises have accompanying audio.
Clicking on the corresponding number on the app will play the relevant audio file.

 Most exercises have accompanying audio. After completing an exercise, the child should listen to the correct answers and then repeat them out loud.

FREE AUDIO
website and app

www.dkefe.com/junior/uk

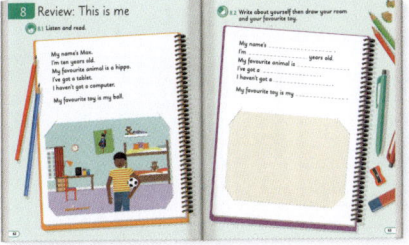

Review units

Four review units provide the child with a chance to read a text incorporating vocabulary and grammar from recent units. The child then writes a personalized answer based on this text.

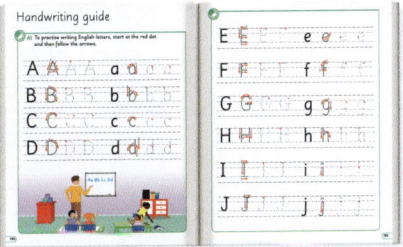

Handwriting guide

The book includes a guide explaining how to form each letter of the English alphabet. The child has space to practise the formation of each letter.

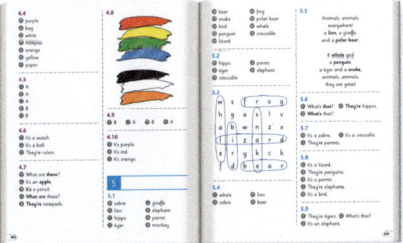

Answers

At the back of the book, answers to all the exercises are clearly presented. Key information is sometimes shown in bold to make it easier to mark the child's work.

Practising new vocabulary

Each unit opens with an illustrated scene that matches the course book, but with the words removed and placed in a panel. The parent or teacher should supervise the child as they listen to the accompanying audio on the website or the app and write the correct words in the spaces.

1 First, click on the corresponding unit number (here **Unit 15**) on your screen. Then, click on the exercise number and play each audio file in turn.

All the words needed to **2** complete the scene are given in a word pool.

3 After listening to each word, the child should write it down in the correct space, using the panel to help them.

4 After completing the scene by writing in all the words, press **Play all** to listen to all the words again.

5 The audio pauses for a few seconds after each word. The child should repeat the word during this pause.

Practising new grammar

Grammar is practised in the same order that it is taught in the corresponding course book unit. Throughout the grammar exercises, vocabulary from the unit is repeated and recycled to help the child memorize it and see it used in context.

1 The child practises the grammar from the corresponding course book unit in exercises that reuse the unit's vocabulary.

2 Use the exercise number (here **15.9**) to find the answers for each exercise at the back of the book, starting on page 199.

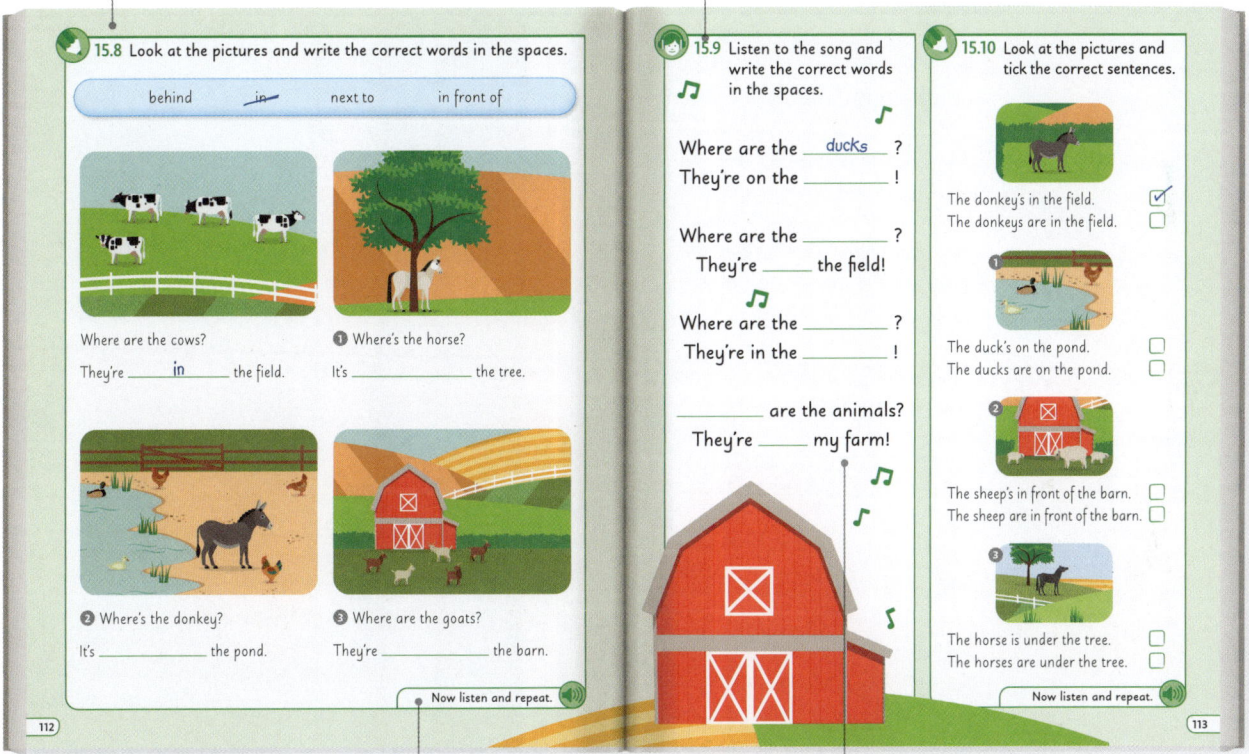

3 Most exercises have an audio recording so the child can listen to the questions and correct answers after completing each exercise.

4 All the songs from the course book are repeated, but with some words removed. The child should listen to the song and write the correct words in the spaces.

1 My friends

Hello, I'm Maria. What's your name?

Hi, I'm Max.

Hello, I'm Ben.

① Maria

② B

③ M

Ben ~~Maria~~ Andy

Sara Sofia Max

Hi, I'm Andy. What's your name?

Hi, my name's Sara.

Hello, my name's Sofia.

④ A _____   ⑤ S _____   ⑥ S _____

1.2 Listen and write the correct words in the spaces.

I'm   Maria   ~~Hello~~   Max   Hello   name's

Hello , my name's Sofia.

1  Hi, my _____ Sara.

2  Hi, I'm _____ .

3  Hi, _____ Andy.

4  Hello, I'm _____ .

5 _____ , I'm Ben.

1.3 Find Max and Sara in the picture.

1.4 Listen and circle the correct names.

Ben / Maria

1. Andy / Sofia

2. Maria / Sara

3. Andy / Max

4. Maria / Sofia

5. Ben / Sofia

1.5 Match the numbers to the correct words.

1 — seven

1 3 — one

2 7   six

3 9   three

4 6   eight

5 10   five

6 8   nine

7 5   ten

Now listen and repeat.

1.6 Listen and colour in the numbers you hear.

73 .18 .62
①   ②

.84 .51 .79
③   ④   ⑤

1.7 Count and write the correct numbers under the pictures.

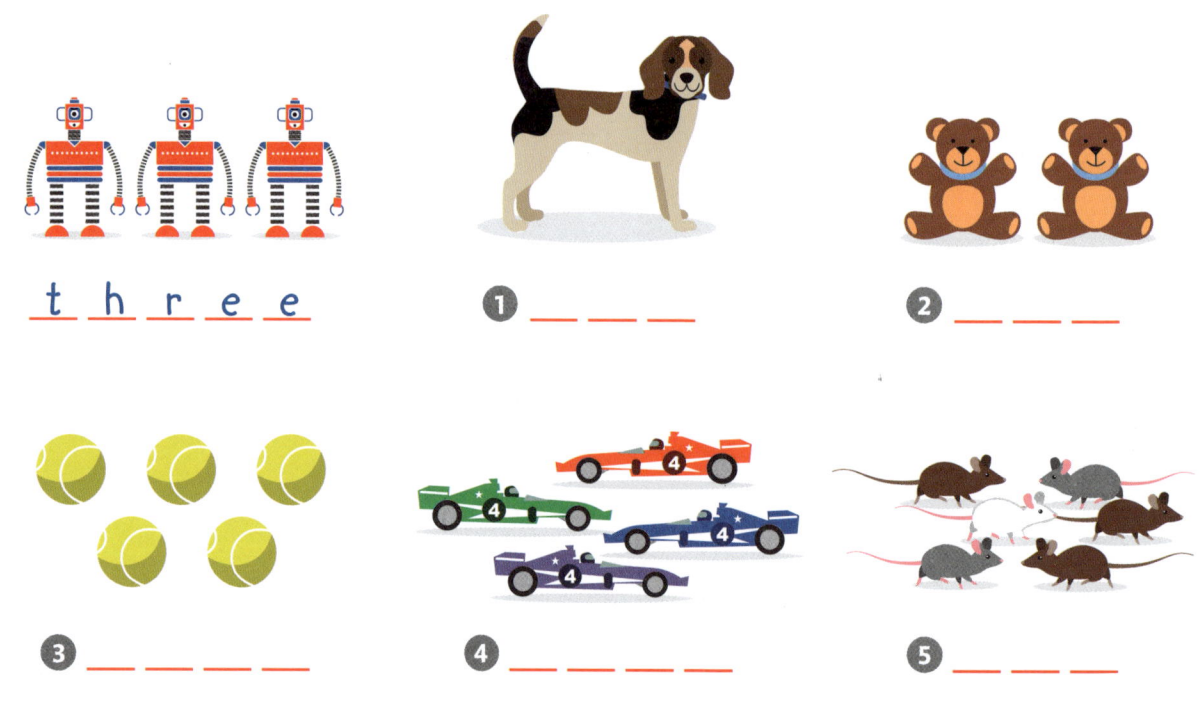

t h r e e

① _ _ _ _

② _ _ _ _

③ _ _ _ _

④ _ _ _ _

⑤ _ _ _ _

Now listen and repeat.

14

1.8 Match the questions to the correct answers.

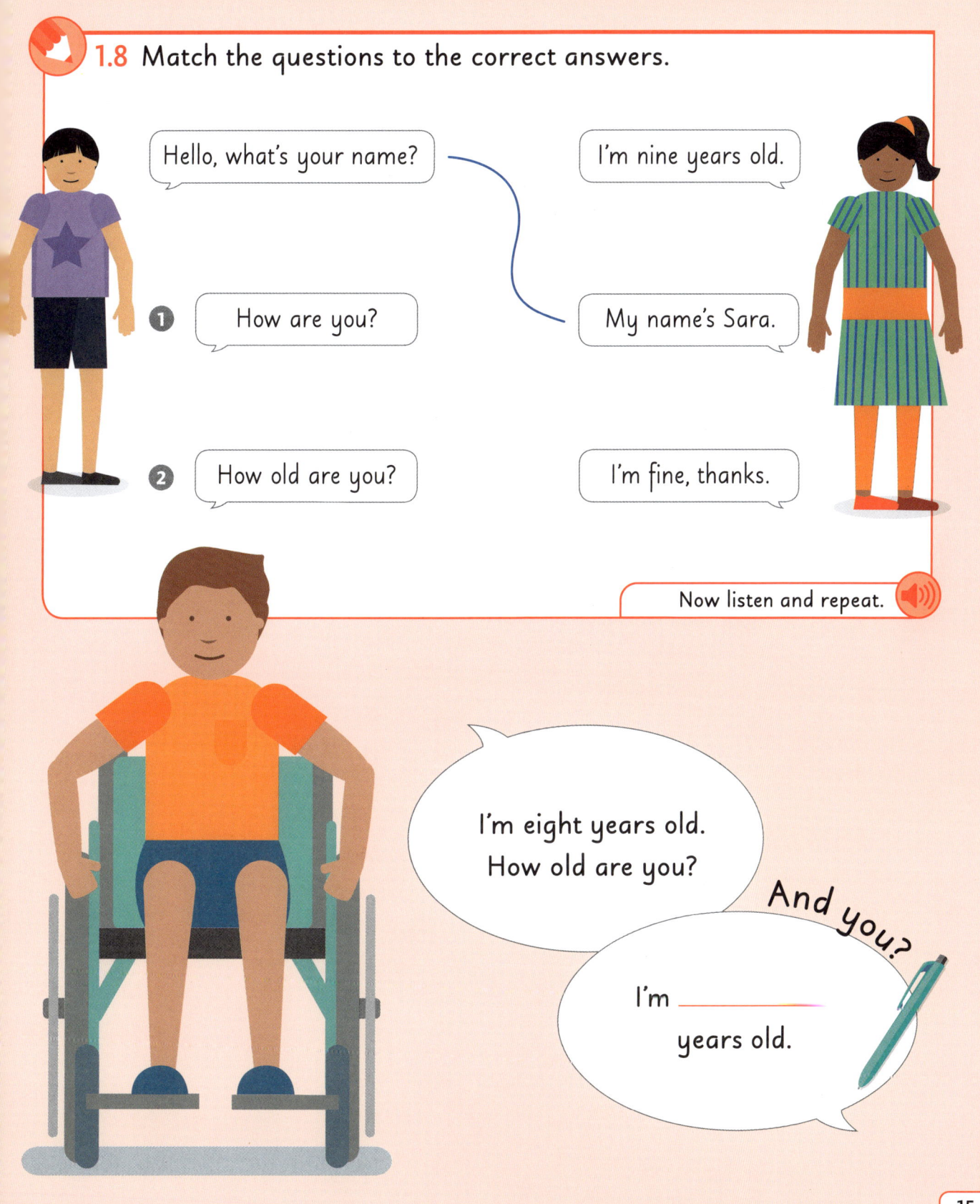

Hello, what's your name?

I'm nine years old.

1 How are you?

My name's Sara.

2 How old are you?

I'm fine, thanks.

Now listen and repeat.

I'm eight years old.
How old are you?

And you?

I'm _____ years old.

2.1 Listen and write the correct words in the spaces.

Sit down, please.

① playground

② n _____

$1\,2\,3\,4\,5\,6\,7\,8\,9\,10$

$1+1$

⑤ b _____

③ l _____

④ t _____

⑥ c _____

7 a_____

8 t_____

9 c_____

10 b_____

letters
teacher
classmate
~~playground~~
numbers
board
tablet
book
alphabet
cupboard

2.2 Look at the pictures and tick the correct words.

numbers ☐
book ☑

1
tablet ☐
board ☐

2
teacher ☐
letters ☐

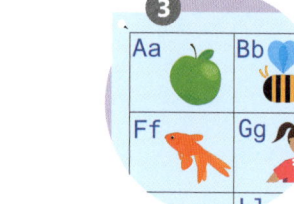
3
cupboard ☐
alphabet ☐

4
board ☐
classmate ☐

5
playground ☐
book ☐

6
numbers ☐
letters ☐

7
numbers ☐
cupboard ☐

8
board ☐
classmate ☐

9
tablet ☐
cupboard ☐

Now listen and repeat.

2.3 Look at the pictures and write the words in the correct place on the crossword.

2.4 Listen and tick the correct pictures.

A ☐   B ☑

①

A ☐   B ☐

②

A ☐   B ☐

③

A ☐   B ☐

④

A ☐   B ☐

⑤

A ☐   B ☐

2.5 Match the pictures to the correct words.

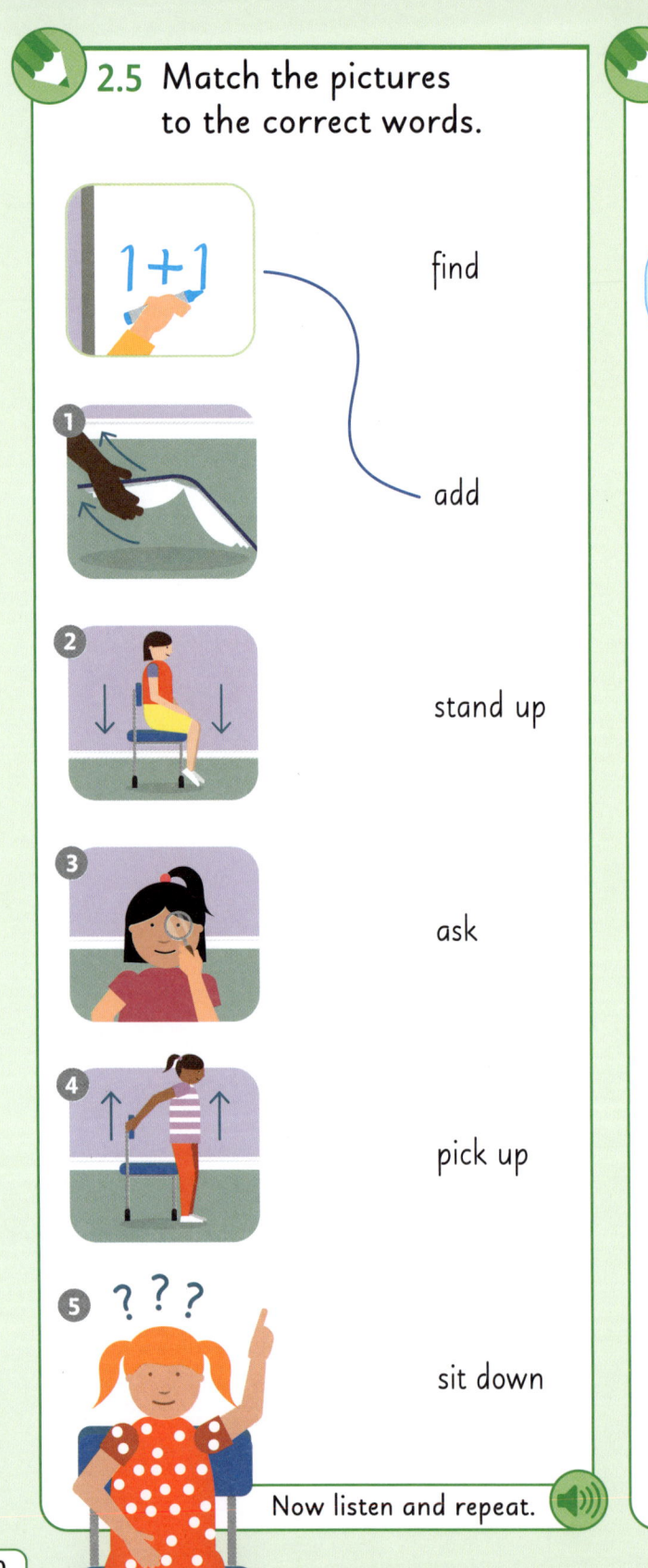

find

add

stand up

ask

pick up

sit down

Now listen and repeat.

2.6 Look at the pictures and write the correct words in the spaces.

| find | close | ~~open~~ |
| answer | show | listen |

open

1

2

3

4

5

Now listen and repeat.

2.7 Look at the pictures and write the letters in the correct order.

l s t i n e

l i s t e n

f d n i

1 f _ _ _ _

a k s

2 a _ _

s o w h

3 s _ _ _

l k o o

4 l _ _ _

o n p e

5 o _ _ _

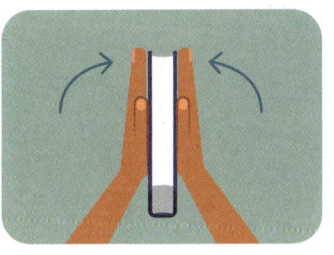

c s o l e

6 c _ _ _ _

d d a

7 a _ _

a r w e s n

8 a _ _ _ _ _

Now listen and repeat.

2.8 Look at the pictures and circle the correct words.

His / (Her) name's Sara.

❶ His / Her name's Andy.

❷ His / Her name's Ben.

❸ His / Her name's Maria.

❹ His / Her name's Max.

❺ His / Her name's Sofia.

Now listen and repeat.

2.9 Listen and match the questions to the correct answers.

What's his name?   Her name's Bella.

1 What's his name?   His name's Tom.

2 What's her name?   Her name's Amy.

3 What's his name?   His name's Ted.

4 What's her name?   His name's Dan.

5 What's her name?   Her name's Anna.

2.10 There are four sentences. Mark the beginning and end of each one and write them below.

What's her name?

1 _____

2 _____

3 _____

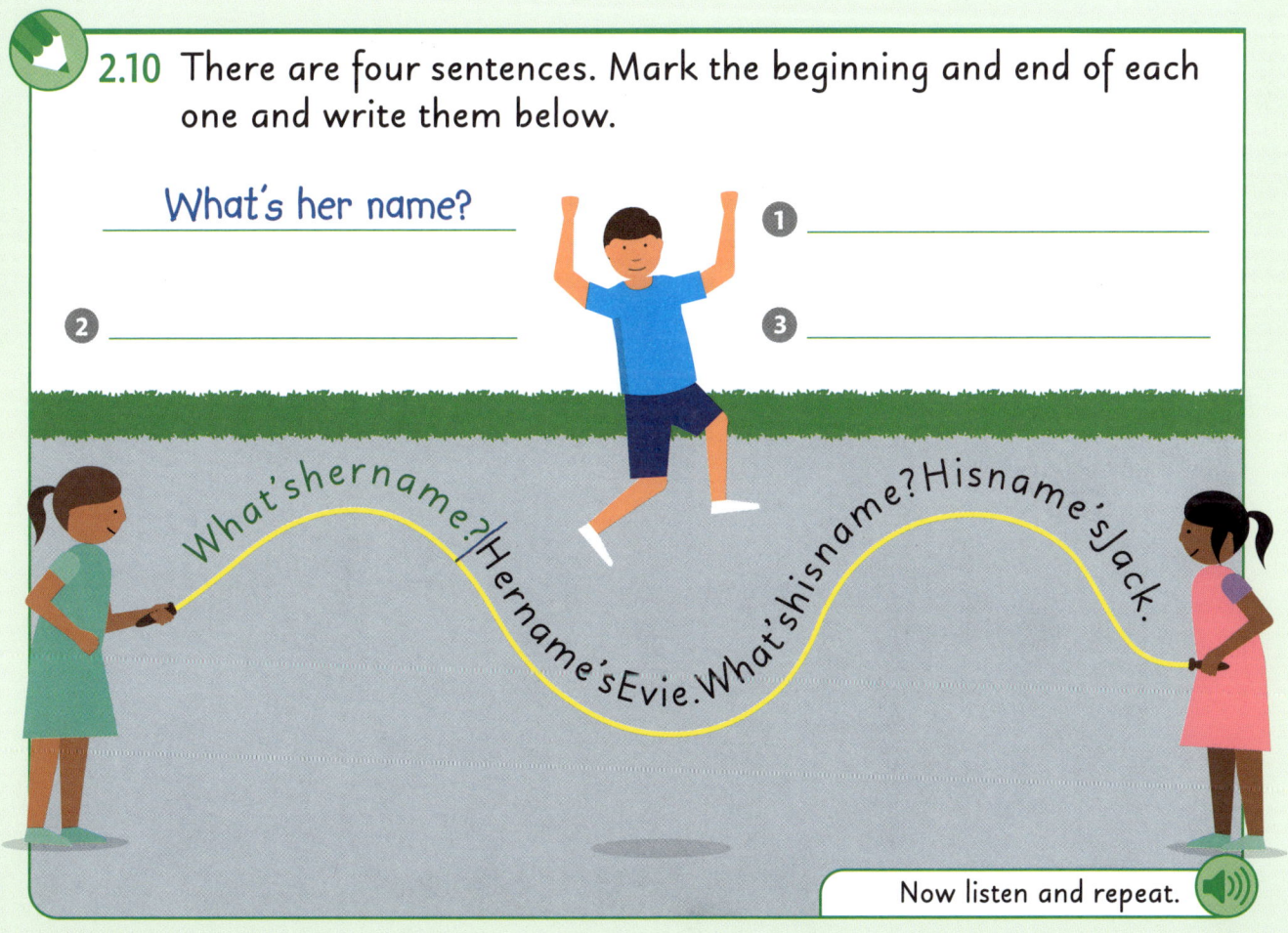

What'shername?|Hername'sEvie.What'shisname?Hisname'sJack.

Now listen and repeat.

23

3 Our classroom

3.1 Listen and write the correct words in the spaces.

3.2 Look at the pictures and circle the correct words.

draw / (count)

read / play

play / spell

draw / write

paint / count

Now listen and repeat.

3.3 Listen and tick the correct pictures.

A ☐   B ✓

❶ A ☐   B ☐

❷ A ☐   B ☐

❸ A ☐   B ☐

❹ A ☐   B ☐

❺ A ☐   B ☐

3.4 Match the pictures to the correct sentences.

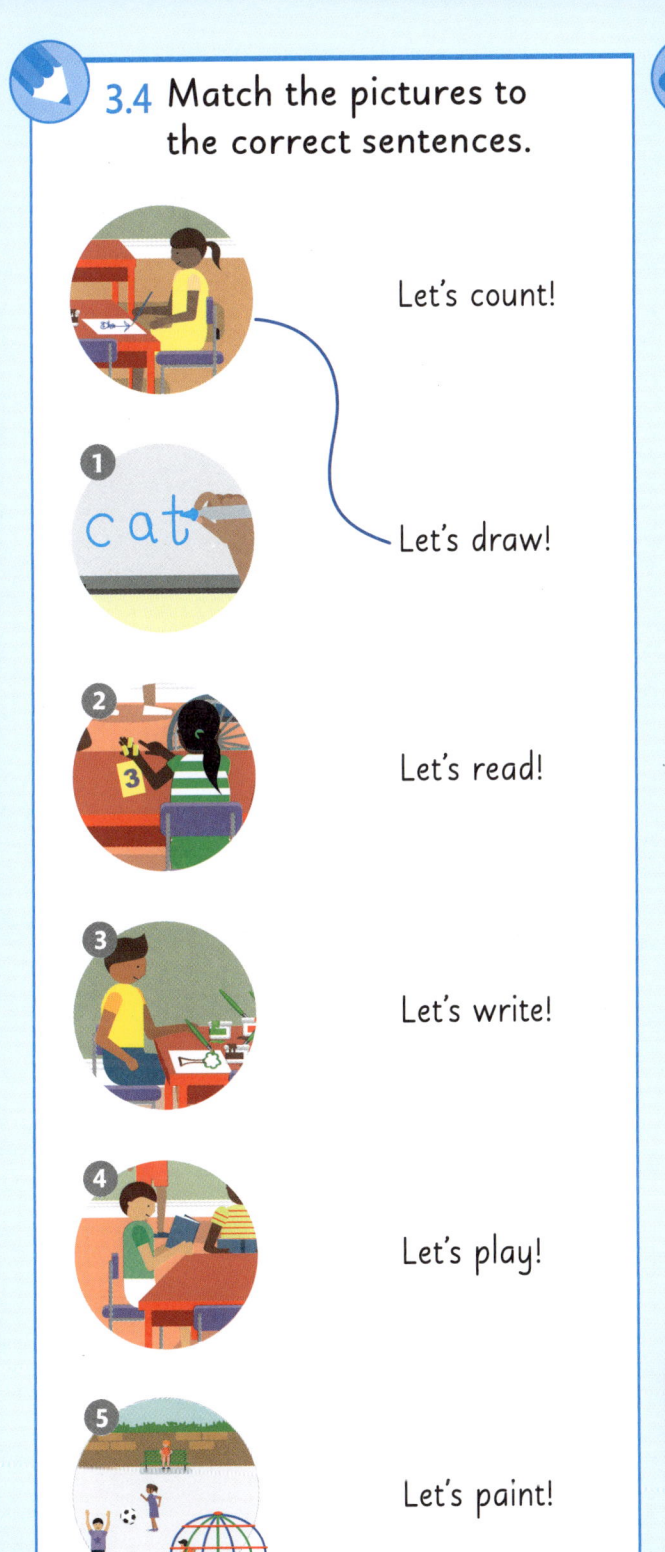

Let's count!

1

Let's draw!

2

Let's read!

3

Let's write!

4

Let's play!

5

Let's paint!

Now listen and repeat.

3.5 Listen to the song and write the correct words in the spaces.

Hello, _hello_ !
What's your _____ ?
How are you?
Let's _____ a game.

_____ say hello
to my new friends
_____ and Maria,
Sara and _____ .

 **3.6** Match the numbers to the correct words.

17 **.12** ① **.16** ② **.15** ③ **.20** ④

sixteen   twenty   fifteen

seventeen   twelve

Now listen and repeat.

 3.7 Write the correct words under the numbers.

eighteen   ~~twelve~~   eleven   fourteen

twenty   thirteen   nineteen   sixteen   fifteen

12   **.14** ①   **.19** ②

twelve

.18 ③   **.11** ④   **.16** ⑤

.20 ⑥   **.13** ⑦   **.15** ⑧

Now listen and repeat.

28

3.8 Look at the pictures and circle the correct words.

book / (books)

1 tablet / tablets

2 number / numbers

3  car / cars

4  dog / dogs

5  cupboard / cupboards

Now listen and repeat.

3.9 Read the words and tick the correct pictures.

pen

A 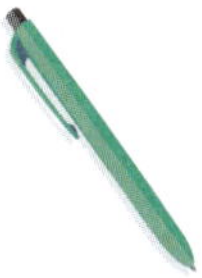 ☐   B ☑

1 cat

A  ☐   B ☐

2 letters

A  ☐   B ☐

3 chair

A  ☐   B ☐

4 dolls

A  ☐   B ☐

Now listen and repeat.

4.1 Listen and write the correct words in the spaces.

crayon   ~~pink~~

book	pen	rubber
ball	paper	notepad
bag	purple	ruler
white	red	brown
green	apple	yellow
orange	pencil	blue
grey	watch	black

① pink _____

② b _____

③ c _____

④ r _____

⑤ p _____

⑥ p _____

⑦ b _____

⑧ n _____

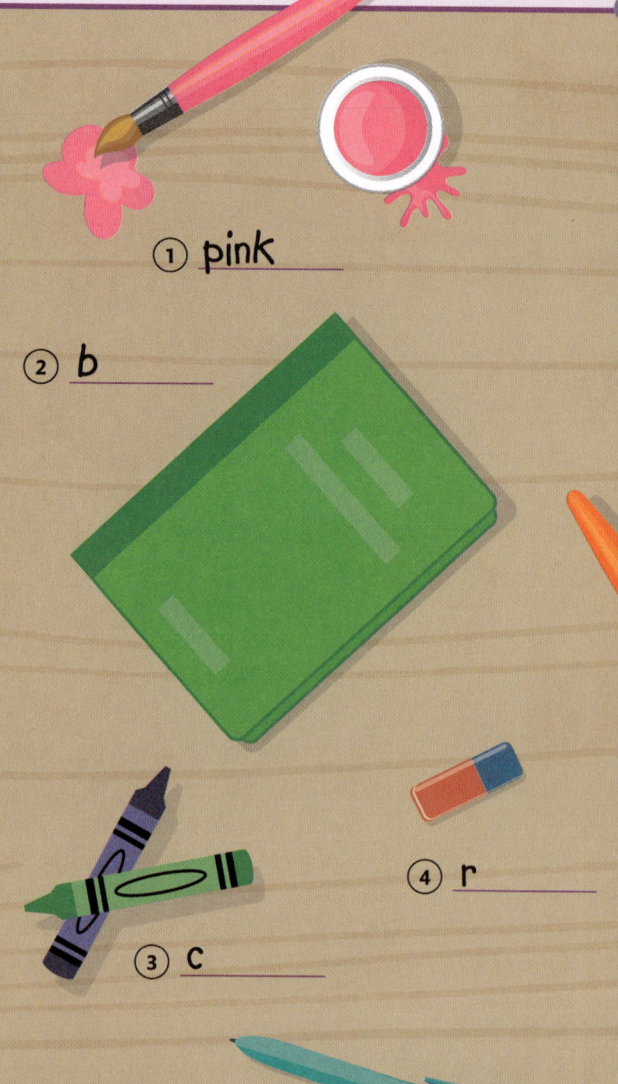

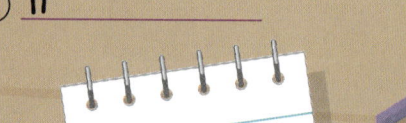

⑩ r _____

⑨ p _____

⑪ b _____

⑫ r _____

⑬ w _____

⑭ b _____

⑮ a _____

⑱ y _____

⑯ o _____

⑰ g _____

⑲ b _____

㉒ b _____

㉑ g _____

⑳ p _____

㉓ w _____

What's this?

It's a pencil.

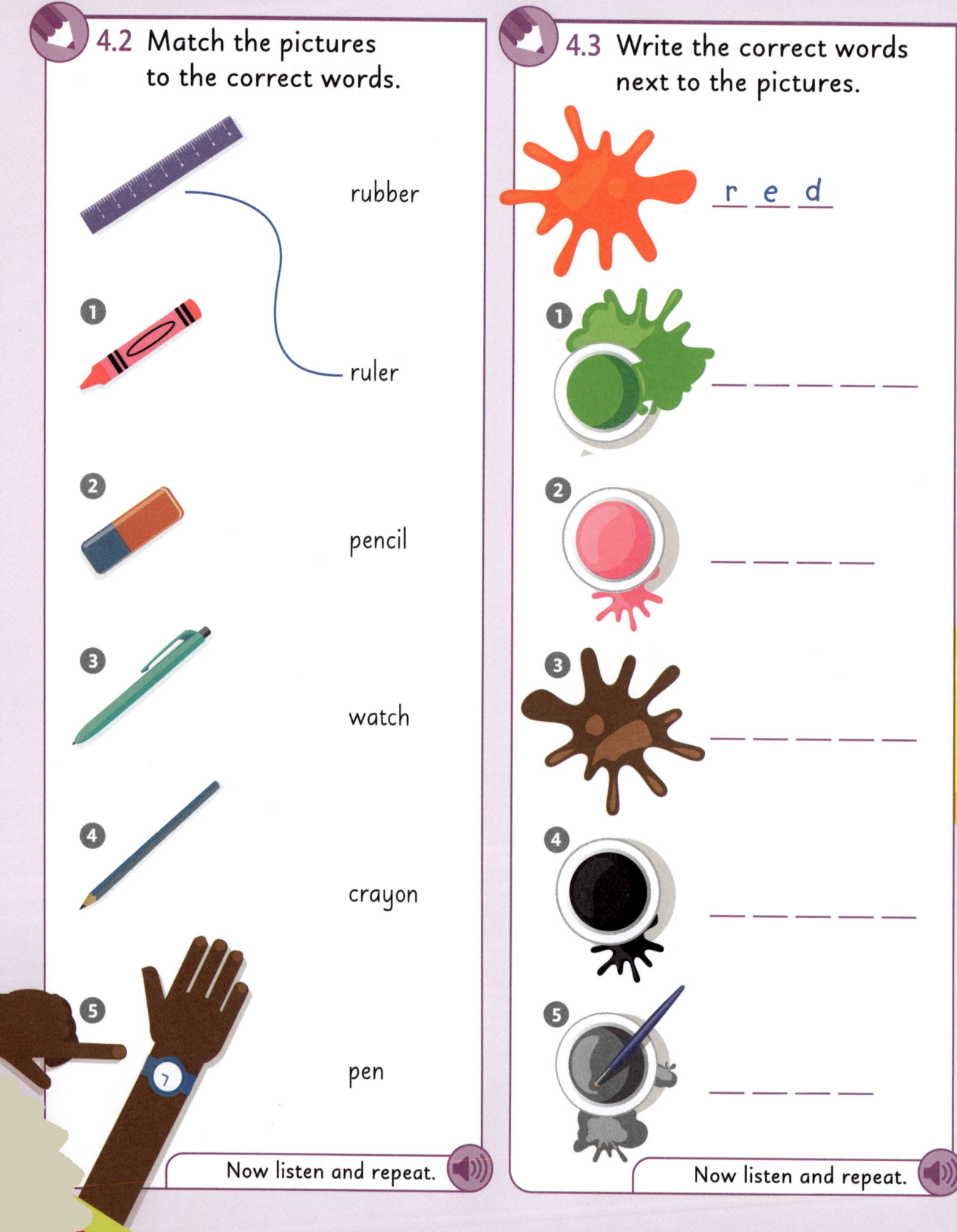

4.2 Match the pictures to the correct words.

rubber

① ruler

② pencil

③ watch

④ crayon

⑤ pen

Now listen and repeat.

4.3 Write the correct words next to the pictures.

<u>r e d</u>

① _ _ _ _ _

② _ _ _ _

③ _ _ _ _ _

④ _ _ _ _

⑤ _ _ _ _

Now listen and repeat.

4.4 Look at the pictures and tick the correct words.

white ☐
blue ✔
pink ☐

1 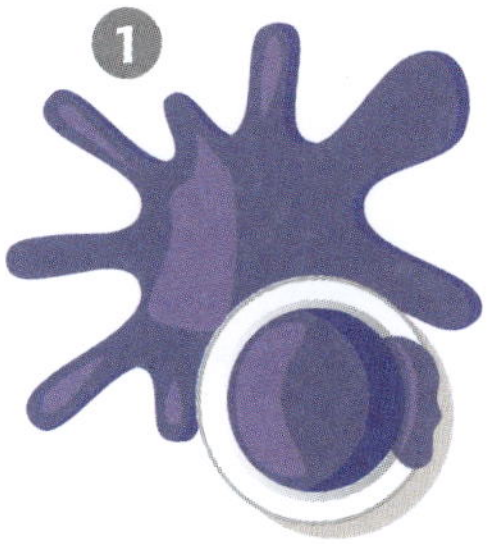
purple ☐
green ☐
crayon ☐

2 
watch ☐
ruler ☐
bag ☐

3 
paper ☐
white ☐
watch ☐

4 
pink ☐
notepad ☐
red ☐

5 
orange ☐
blue ☐
apple ☐

6 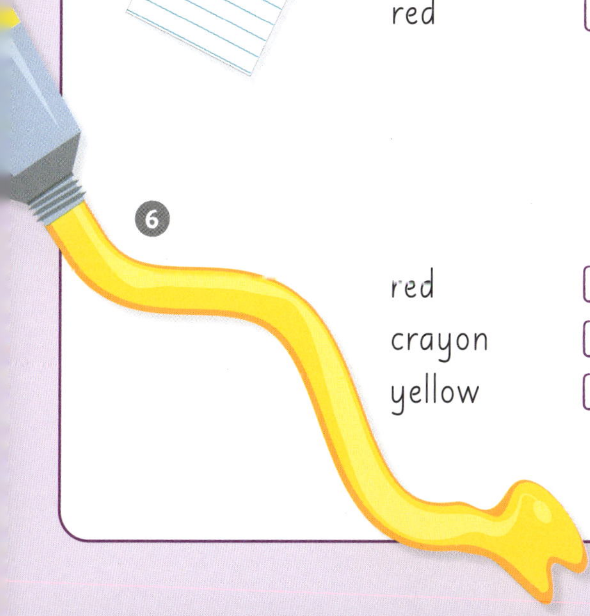
red ☐
crayon ☐
yellow ☐

7 
paper ☐
brown ☐
pencil ☐

Now listen and repeat. 🔊

4.5 Listen and tick the correct pictures.

A ✓ B ☐

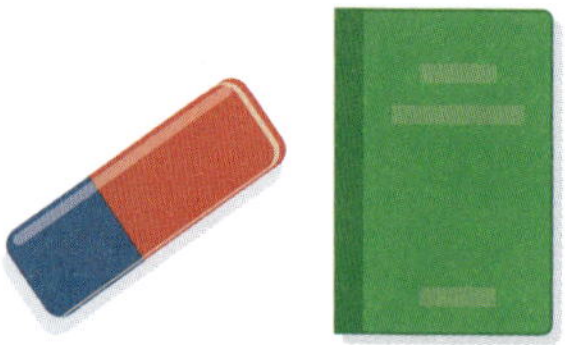

① A ☐ B ☐

② A ☐ B ☐

③ A ☐ B ☐

④ A ☐ B ☐

⑤ A ☐ B ☐

4.6 Look at the pictures and write the correct answers in the spaces.

It's a ball.   ~~They're books.~~

It's a watch.   They're rulers.

What are these?

They're books.

① What's this?

_____

② What's this?

_____

③ What are these?

_____

Now listen and repeat.

4.7 Look at the pictures and write the correct words in the spaces.

It's   What are   They're   ~~What's~~   these   apple

What's this?

It's a ruler.

1 What are _____ ?

They're crayons.

2 What's this?

It's an _____ .

3 What's this?

_____ a pencil.

4 _____ these?

They're books.

5 What are these?

_____ notepads.

Now listen and repeat.

4.8 Listen to the song and colour in the picture.

Red,

yellow,

green,

and blue!

Black

white, and

orange, too!

4.9 Listen and tick the correct pictures.

A ☐   B ☑

1   A ☐   B ☐

2   A ☐   B ☐

3   A ☐   B ☐

4   A ☐   B ☐

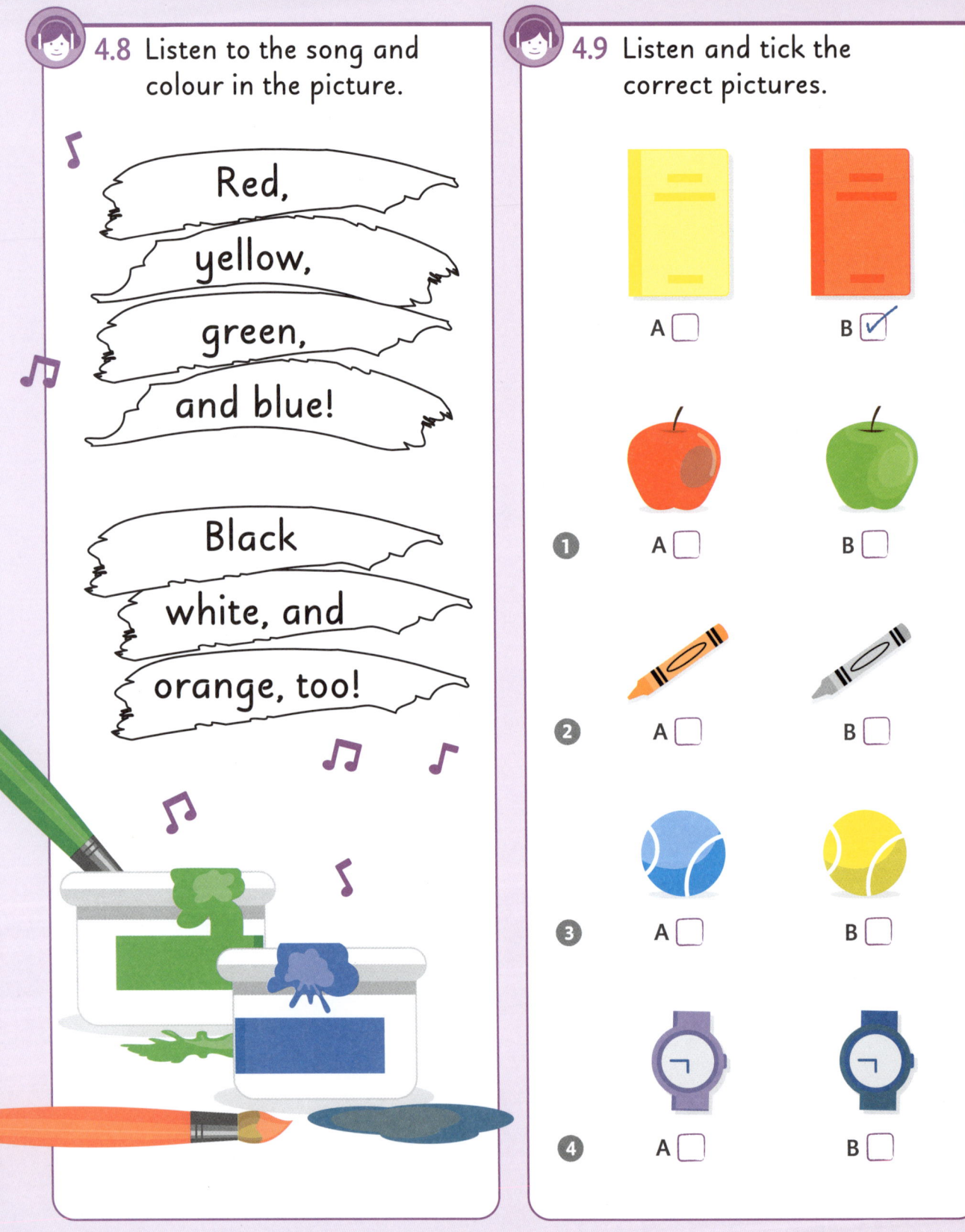

4.10 Look at the picture and match the questions to the correct answers.

What colour is the book? — It's red.

1. What colour is the bag? — It's blue.

2. What colour is the apple? — It's orange.

3. What colour is the ball? — It's purple.

Now listen and repeat.

5 Our favourite animals

5.1 Listen and write the correct words in the spaces.

① zebra

② g

③ l

④ e

⑤ h

⑥ p

⑦ t

⑧ m

⑨ b

⑩ f

⑪ s

12 p _____

13 b _____

14 w _____

15 p _____

16 c _____

17 l _____

It's a crocodile!

What's that?

lion
hippo
zebra
elephant
giraffe
tiger
bear
monkey
parrot
snake
frog
whale
polar bear
bird
crocodile
lizard
penguin

5.2 Look at the pictures and circle the correct words.

giraffe / (frog)

1 hippo / polar bear

2 lion / parrot

3 tiger / snake

4 bear / elephant

5 crocodile / bird

Now listen and repeat.

5.3 Find and circle the five words in the grid.

bear

lizard

~~snake~~

whale

frog

bird

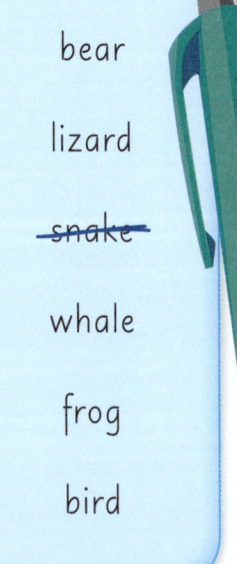

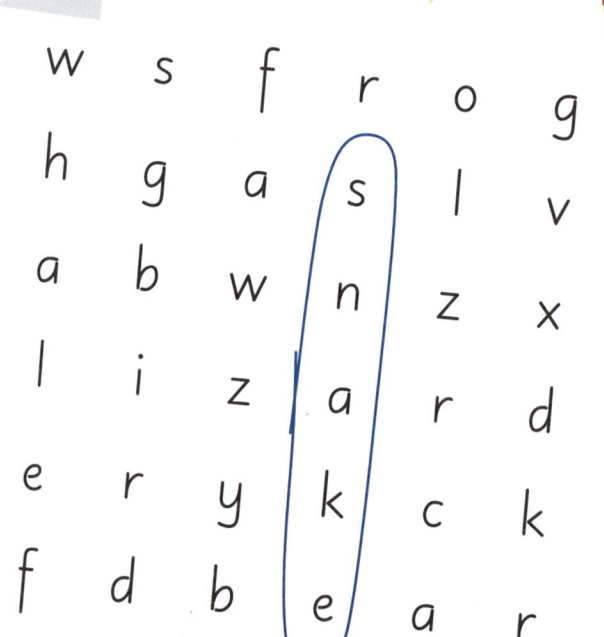

w	s	f	r	o	g
h	g	a	s	l	v
a	b	w	n	z	x
l	i	z	a	r	d
e	r	y	k	c	k
f	d	b	e	a	r

40

5.4 Look at the pictures and write the letters in the correct order.

s a k n e

s n a k e

1. w l h a e

w _ _ _ _ _

2. l o n i

l _ _ _ _

3. z b a e r

z _ _ _ _ _

4. b r a e

b _ _ _ _

Now listen and repeat.

5.5 Listen to the song and write the correct words in the spaces.

Animals, animals everywhere!
A ___lion___ , a giraffe, and a _____ .

A _____ and a _____ ,
a tiger and a _____ ,
animals, animals,
they are great!

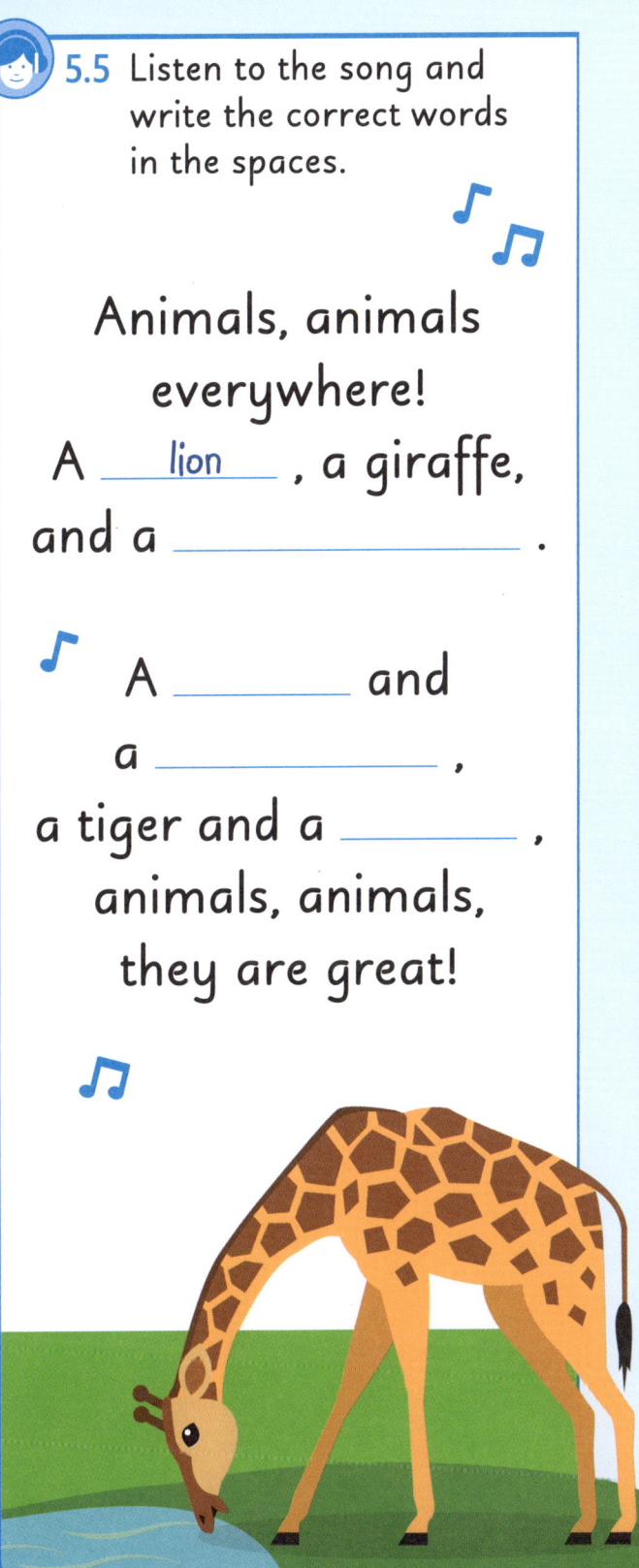

5.6 Look at the pictures and write the correct words in the spaces.

What's   that   They're   ~~frog~~

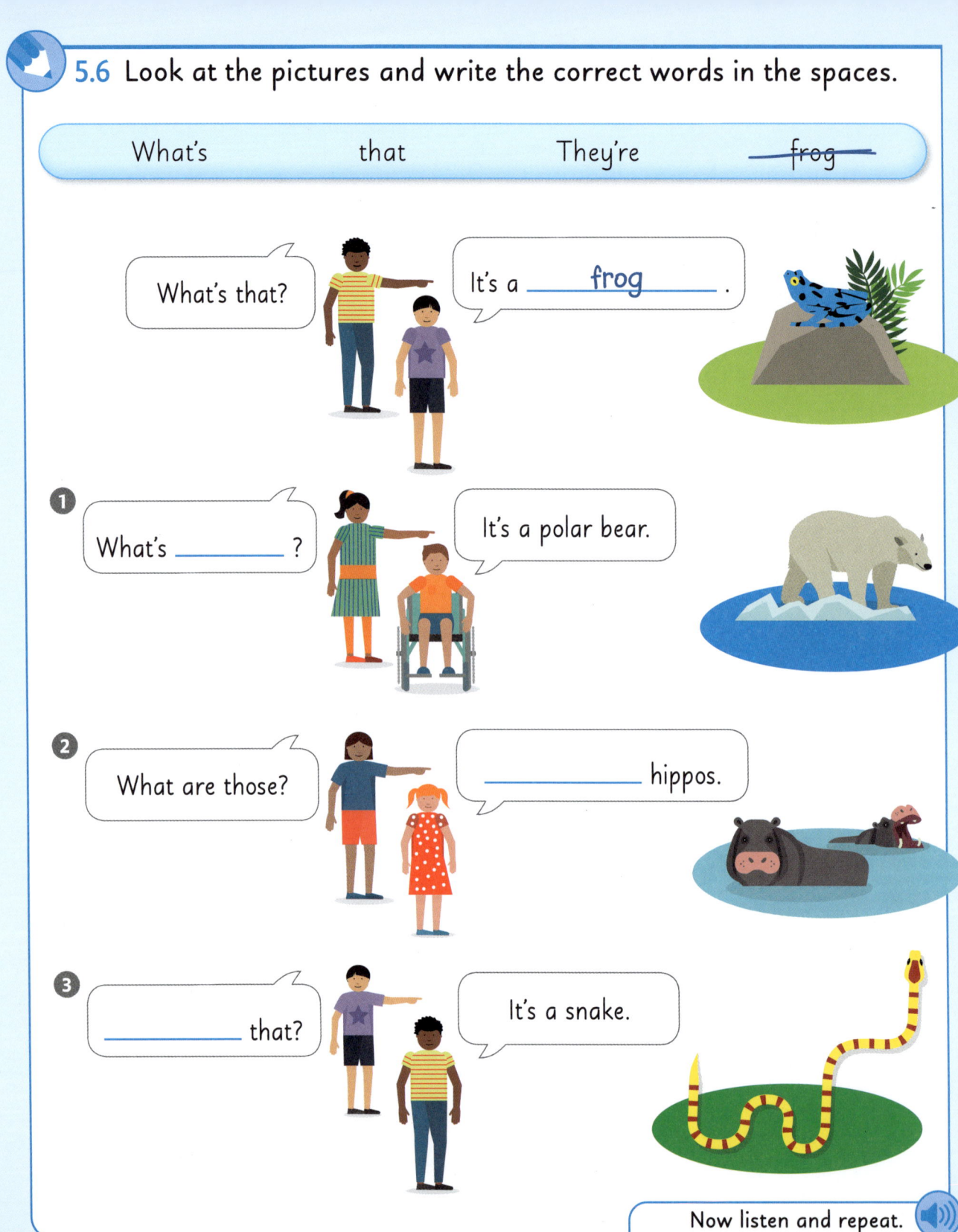

What's that?

It's a _____ frog _____.

1 What's _____?

It's a polar bear.

2 What are those?

_____ hippos.

3 _____ that?

It's a snake.

Now listen and repeat.

5.7 Look at the pictures and write the correct answers in the spaces.

It's a crocodile.   ~~They're monkeys.~~
    They're parrots.   It's a zebra.

What are those?
They're monkeys.

1 What's that?
_____

2 What's that?
_____

3 What are those?
_____

Now listen and repeat.

5.8 Listen and match the questions to the correct answers.

What are those?   It's a lizard.

1 What's that?   It's a bird.

2 What are those?   They're elephants.

3 What's that?   They're lions.

4 What are those?   It's a parrot.

5 What's that?   They're penguins.

5.9 There are four sentences. Mark the beginning and end of each one and write them below.

Whatarethose? | They'retigers. What'sthat? It'sanelephant.

What are those?

1 _____

2 _____   3 _____

Now listen and repeat.

5.10 Listen and tick the correct pictures.

A ☐   B ☑   1 A ☐   B ☐   2 A ☐   B ☐

3 A ☐   B ☐   4 A ☐   B ☐   5 A ☐   B ☐

5.11 Look at the pictures and write the correct words in the spaces.

bird ~~frog~~ monkey bear elephant lizard

 What's your favourite animal?  My favourite animal is a _frog_ .

1  What's your favourite animal?  My favourite animal is a _____ .

2  What's your favourite animal?  My favourite animal is a _____ .

3  What's your favourite animal?  My favourite animal is a _____ .

4  What's your favourite animal?  My favourite animal is an _____ .

5  What's your favourite animal?  My favourite animal is a _____ .

Now listen and repeat.

This is my family

6.1 Listen and write the correct words in the spaces.

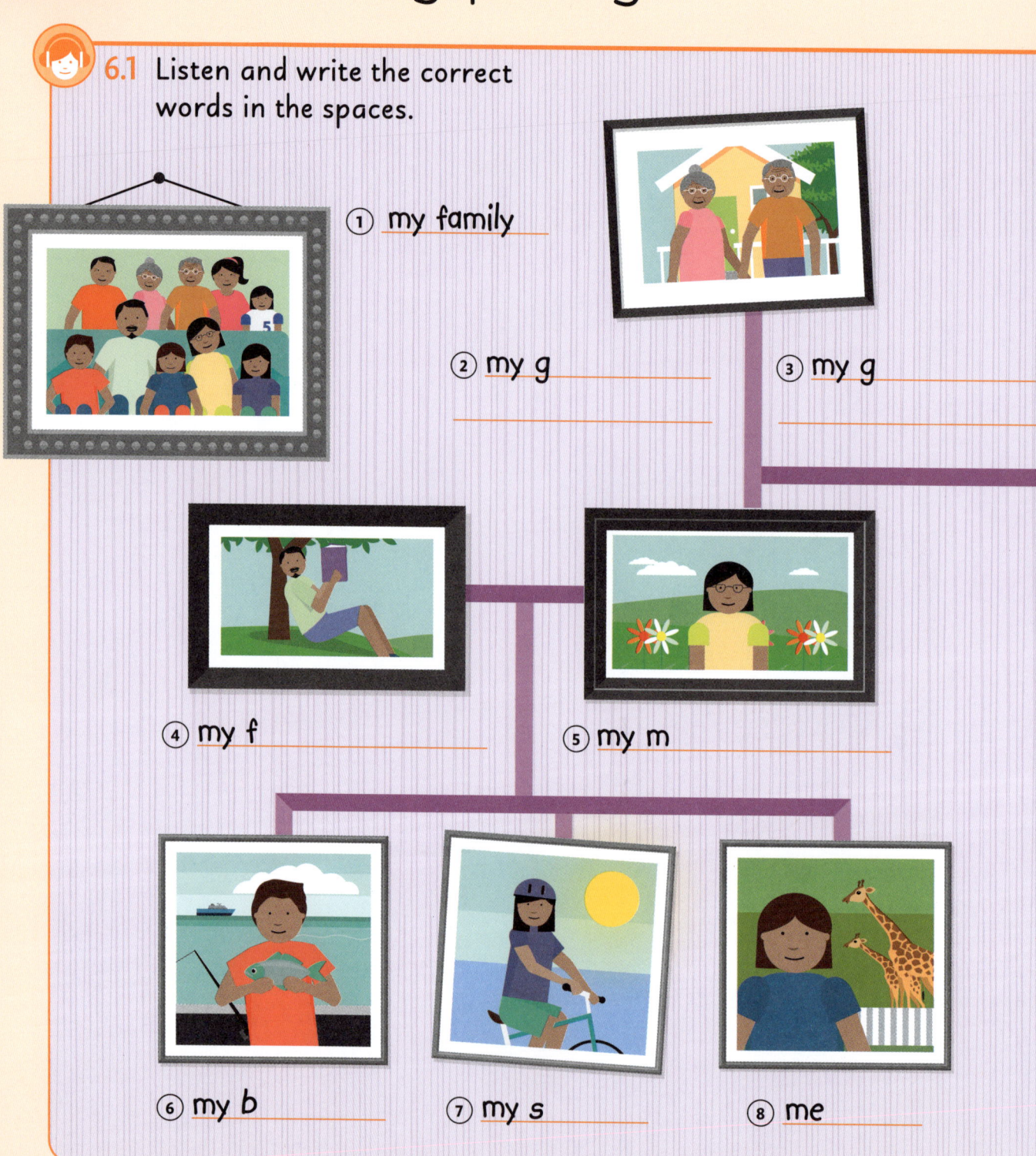

① my family

② my g _____

③ my g _____

④ my f _____

⑤ my m _____

⑥ my b _____

⑦ my s _____

⑧ me

~~my family~~   my mother / mum   ~~me~~

my grandmother / grandma   my brother   my aunt

my father / dad   my sister   my uncle

my cousin   my grandfather / grandpa

⑨ my u _____

⑩ my a _____

Who's that?

She's my cousin.

⑪ my c _____

6.2 Match the pictures to the correct words.

my cousin

1

my dad

2

my uncle

3

my grandma

4

my grandpa

5

my family

Now listen and repeat.

6.3 Look at the pictures and tick the correct words.

aunt ✔
uncle
grandmother

1 
sister
aunt
brother

2 
cousin
mother
father

3 
grandma
sister
grandfather

4 
sister
grandpa
uncle

Now listen and repeat.

6.4 Look at the pictures and write the correct words in the spaces.

grandma ~~brother~~ uncle cousin sister dad

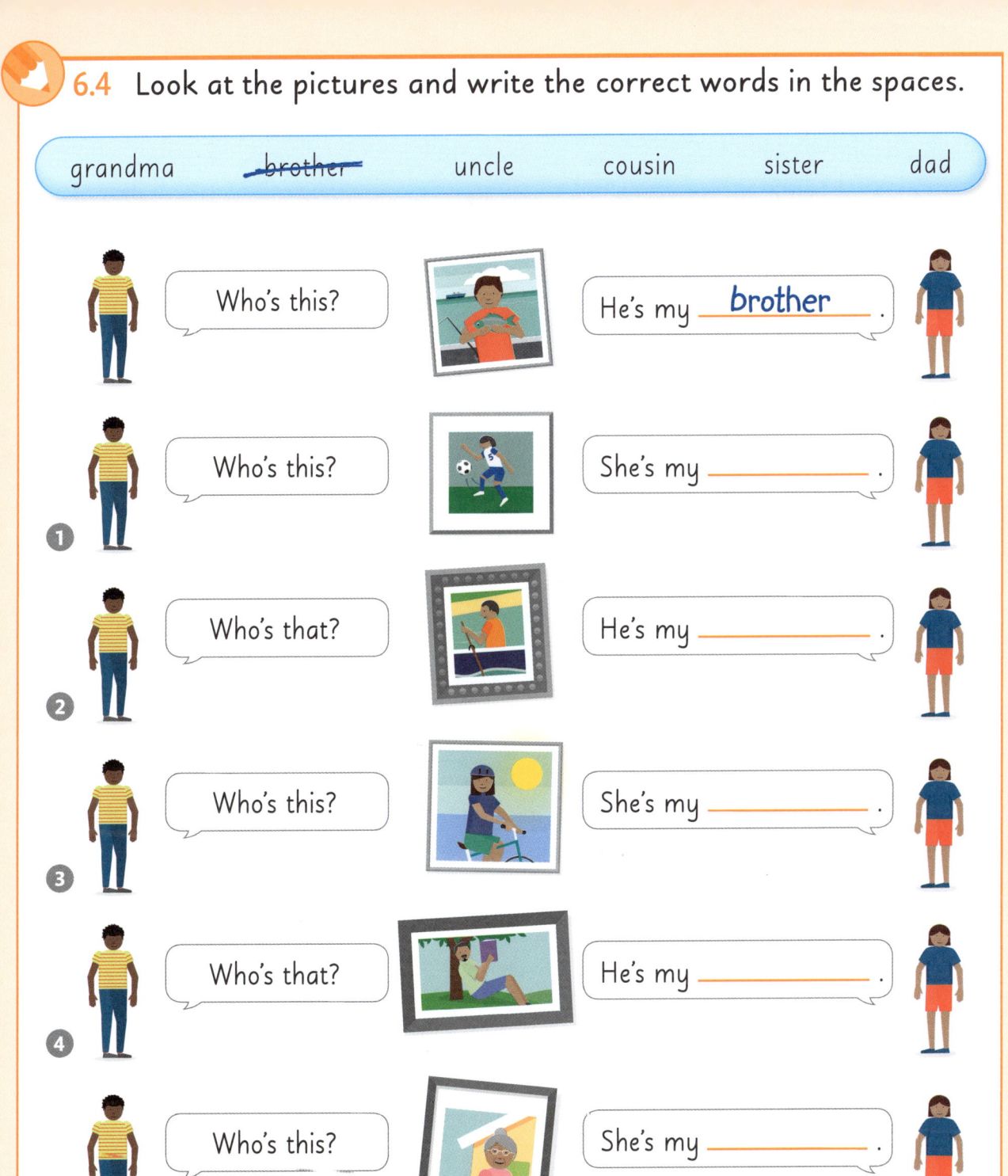

Who's this?

He's my brother.

1 Who's this?

She's my _____.

2 Who's that?

He's my _____.

3 Who's this?

She's my _____.

4 Who's that?

He's my _____.

5 Who's this?

She's my _____.

Now listen and repeat.

6.5 Listen and tick the correct answers.

Is he your dad?

Yes, he is. ✔

No, he isn't. ☐

1 Is he your brother?

Yes, he is. ☐

No, he isn't. ☐

2 Is she your sister?

Yes, she is. ☐

No, she isn't. ☐

3 Is she your mother?

Yes, she is. ☐

No, she isn't. ☐

6.6 Match the pictures to the correct words.

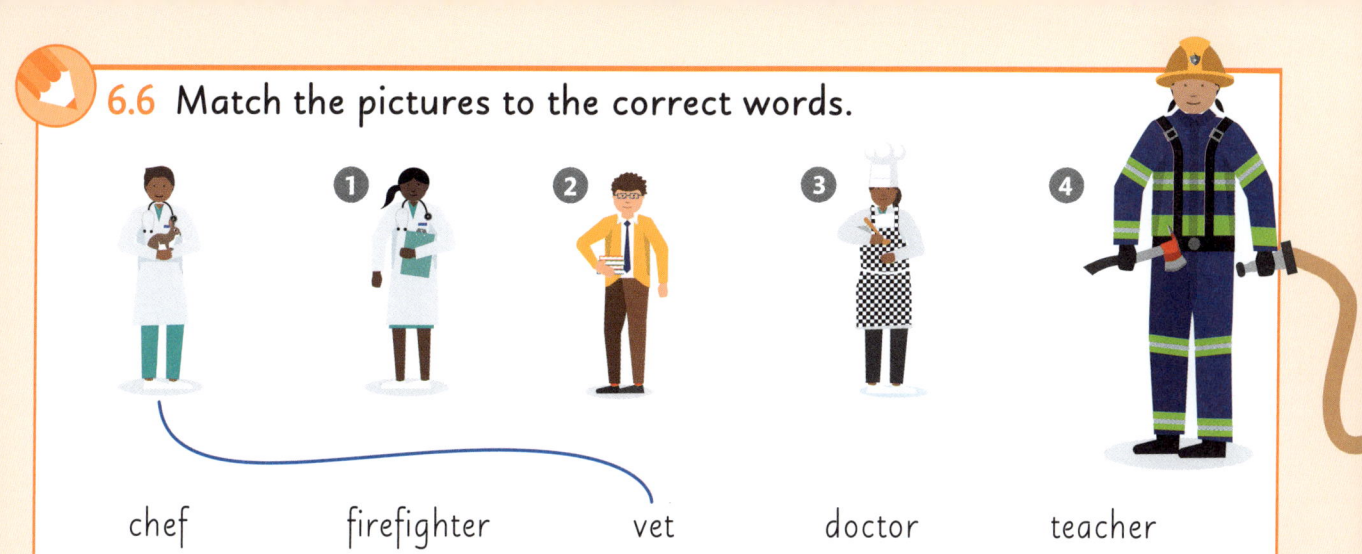

chef　　　　firefighter　　　　vet　　　　doctor　　　　teacher

Now listen and repeat.

6.7 Find and circle the four words in the grid.

teacher　　　　vet　　　　~~doctor~~　　　　farmer　　　　chef

d o c t o r g f
t v y i j w r a
t e a c h e r r
f t r h y f h m
a q g l m b q e
w c h e f d m r

6.8 Look at the pictures and write the correct words in the spaces.

teacher   ~~farmer~~   chef

doctor   police officer

He's a __farmer__ .

1 She's a _____ .

2 He's a _____ .

3 She's a _____ .

4 She's a _____ .

Now listen and repeat.

6.9 Look at the pictures and tick the correct sentences.

He's a firefighter. ✔
She's a firefighter. ☐

1. He's a doctor. ☐
   She's a doctor. ☐

2. She's a chef. ☐
   He's a chef. ☐

3. He's a farmer. ☐
   She's a farmer. ☐

4. He's a teacher. ☐
   She's a teacher. ☐

5. She's a police officer. ☐
   He's a police officer. ☐

Now listen and repeat.

6.10 Listen to the song and write the correct words in the spaces.

Who's this?
She's my _____mother_____.
Who's that?
He's my _____.

My _____ is a teacher,
my _____ is a vet,
Grandpa's a _____,
and Grandma's a _____!

5   53

7 This is my room

Listen and write the correct words in the spaces.

① poster

② c

③ m

④ k

⑤ l

⑥ t

⑦ d

⑧ d

⑨ c

⑩ c

⑪ c

⑫ r

These are my toys.

This is my camera.

13　b _____

14　t _____

15　b _____

16　b _____

17　s _____

18　t _____

lamp
computer
desk
~~poster~~
keyboard
toy box
rug
mouse
doll
car
bed
chair
skateboard
camera
baseball bat
tennis racket
teddy bear
ball

7.2 Match the pictures to the correct words.

skateboard

1

doll

2

car

3

lamp

4

chair

5

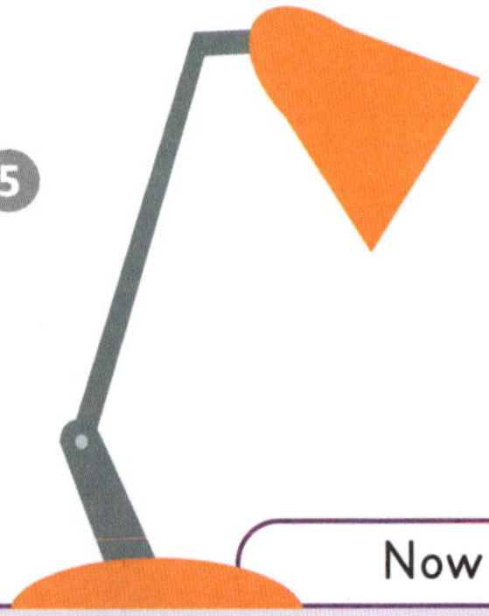

toy box

Now listen and repeat.

7.3 Listen and tick the correct pictures.

A ☐   B ☑

1   A ☐   B ☐

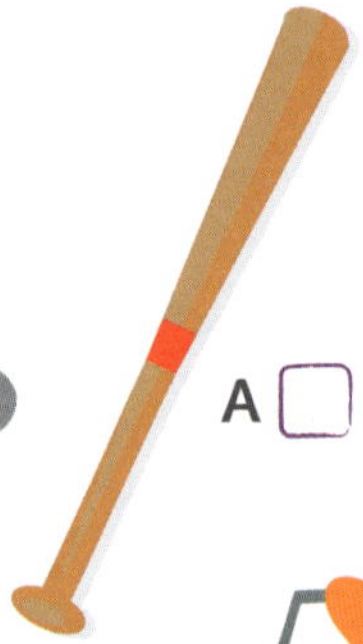

2   A ☐   B ☐

3   A ☐   B ☐

4   A ☐   B ☐

7.4 Read the sentences and tick the correct pictures.

This is my teddy bear. 
A ☐ B ✓

1 These are my cars. 
A ☐ B ☐

2 This is my camera. 
A ☐ B ☐

3 This is my computer. 
A ☐ B ☐

4 These are my dolls. 
A ☐ B ☐

5 This is my ball. 
A ☐ B ☐

Now listen and repeat. 🔊

7.5 Listen and match the names to the correct pictures.

Ben **1** Anna **2** Jack **3** Emma **4** Harry

car

computer

doll

skateboard

toy box

7.6 Look at the pictures and write the correct words in the spaces.

Those are   That's   ~~This is~~   That's

This is   These are

This is _____ my doll.

1 _____ my ball.

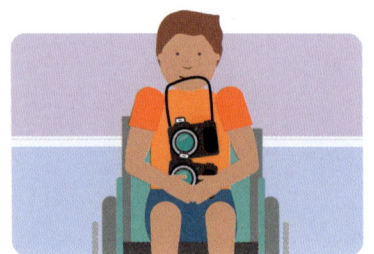

2 _____ my cameras.

3 _____ my teddy bears.

4 _____ my toy box.

5 _____ my tennis racket.

Now listen and repeat.

7.7 Look at the pictures and write the correct names in the spaces.

Maria

Andy

I've got a computer.

Maria

1 I've got a rug.

2 I haven't got a doll.

3 I haven't got a chair.

4 I've got a skateboard.

5 I haven't got a lamp.

6 I've got a teddy bear.

7 I haven't got a car.

Now listen and repeat.

7.8 Listen and write the correct answers below.

Yes, I have.   ~~No, I haven't.~~   No, I haven't.

No, I haven't.   Yes, I have.

Have you got a baseball bat?

 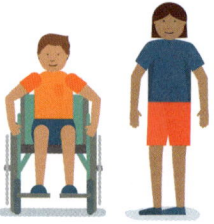

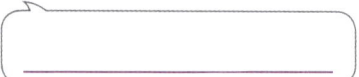 No, I haven't.

1 Have you got a car?

 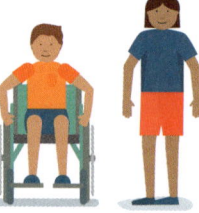

2 Have you got a chair?

3 Have you got a lamp?

4 Have you got a desk?

 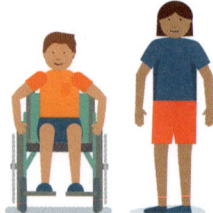

7.9 Look at the pictures and tick the correct answers.

Have you got a car?
Yes, I have. ☐
No, I haven't. ☑

1 Have you got a rug?
Yes, I have. ☐
No, I haven't. ☐

2 Have you got a ball?
Yes, I have. ☐
No, I haven't. ☐

3 Have you got a poster?
Yes, I have. ☐
No, I haven't. ☐

4 Have you got a doll?
Yes, I have. ☐
No, I haven't. ☐

5 Have you got a desk?
Yes, I have. ☐
No, I haven't. ☐

Now listen and repeat.

7.10 Listen to the song and write the correct words in the spaces.

This is my ___toy box___
and these are my _____ ,
I've got a _____
and a _____ , too.
Toys are fantastic!
Toys are cool!

8 Review: This is me

My name's Max.
I'm ten years old.
My favourite animal is a hippo.
I've got a tablet.
I haven't got a computer.

My favourite toy is my ball.

8.2 Write about yourself then draw your room
and your favourite toy.

My name's _____ .
I'm _____ years old.
My favourite animal is _____ .
I've got a _____ .
I haven't got a _____ .

My favourite toy is my _____ .

9 At the fair

Listen and write the correct words in the spaces.

hungry
~~tired~~
thirsty
cold
scared
hot
happy
excited
sad

① tired

② h _____

They're hungry.

We aren't hungry. We're thirsty.

③ t _____

④ s _____

⑤ h _____ ⑥ c _____

⑦ e _____

⑧ s _____ ⑨ h _____

9.2 Look at the pictures and circle the correct words.

excited / (tired)

cold / hungry

scared / excited

thirsty / hungry

sad / tired

happy / hot

Now listen and repeat.

 9.3 Listen and tick the correct pictures.

A ☐   B ☑

1 A ☐   B ☐

2 A ☐   B ☐

3 A ☐   B ☐

4 A ☐   B ☐

5 A ☐   B ☐

9.4 Look at the pictures and write the correct words next to the pictures.

happy   ~~cold~~   tired
excited   thirsty

cold

1. _____

2. _____

3. _____

4. _____

Now listen and repeat.

9.5 Listen to the song and write the correct words in the spaces.

Are you __happy__ ?
_____ , we are!
We are at the fair.

Are you _____ ?
_____ , we aren't.
We aren't tired
or _____ !

9.6 Match the pictures to the correct sentences.

We're thirsty.   We're very scared.   We're really hot.   We're happy.

Now listen and repeat.

9.7 Listen and tick the correct sentences.

We're excited. ✓
They're excited. ☐

1. We're happy. ☐
They're happy. ☐

2. We're cold. ☐
They're cold. ☐

3. We're hot. ☐
They're hot. ☐

4. We're sad. ☐
They're sad. ☐

5. We're thirsty. ☐
They're thirsty. ☐

6. We're tired. ☐
They're tired. ☐

7. We're scared. ☐
They're scared. ☐

9.8 Look at the pictures and write the correct words in the spaces.

hot   ~~thirsty~~   really   happy   excited

They're very ___thirsty___ .

❶ We're really _____ .

❷ They're _____ .

❸ We're _____ .

❹ We're _____ tired.

Now listen and repeat.

69

9.9 Look at the pictures and tick the correct answers.

Are they excited?

Yes, they are. ☐
No, they're not. ☑

❶ Are you scared?

Yes, we are. ☐
No, we're not. ☐

❷ Are you hot?

Yes, we are. ☐
No, we're not. ☐

❸ Are they cold?

Yes, they are. ☐
No, they're not. ☐

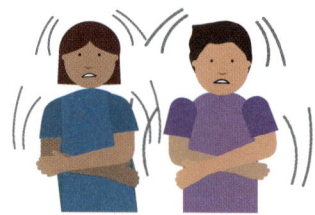

❹ Are you tired?

Yes, we are. ☐
No, we're not. ☐

❺ Are they sad?

Yes, they are. ☐
No, they're not. ☐

Now listen and repeat. 🔊

9.10 Listen and match the questions to the correct answers.

Are you sad?   Yes, they are.

❶ Are they happy?   No, we're not.

❷ Are you excited?   No, they're not.

❸ Are you hungry?   No, we're not.

❹ Are they scared?   Yes, we are.

9.11 Look at the pictures and write the correct answers in the spaces.

No, we're not.   Yes, they are.   ~~Yes, we are.~~   No, they're not.

Yes, they are.   No, we're not.   No, they're not.   Yes, we are.

Are you cold?

Yes, we are.

1 Are they hungry?

2 Are you happy?

3 Are they thirsty?

4 Are they excited?

5 Are you scared?

6 Are you excited?

7 Are they happy?

Now listen and repeat.

71

10 Our pets

dog
collar
~~rabbit~~
mouse
tortoise
vet
spider
cat
fish

Look! Andy's got a dog.

Yes, it's very dirty.

① rabbit

② t

③ d

④ m

⑤ c

6 S _____

7 C _____

8 V _____

9 f _____

10.2 Look at the pictures and write the correct words in the spaces.

scary ~~young~~ dirty old big
nice small clean beautiful

young

1 o

2 n

3 s

4 d

5 c

6 b

7 b

8 s

Now listen and repeat.

10.3 Look at the pictures and tick the correct words.

cat ☐
tortoise ✔

1 dog ☐
rabbit ☐

2 fish ☐
rabbit ☐

3 spider ☐
vet ☐

4 cat ☐
collar ☐

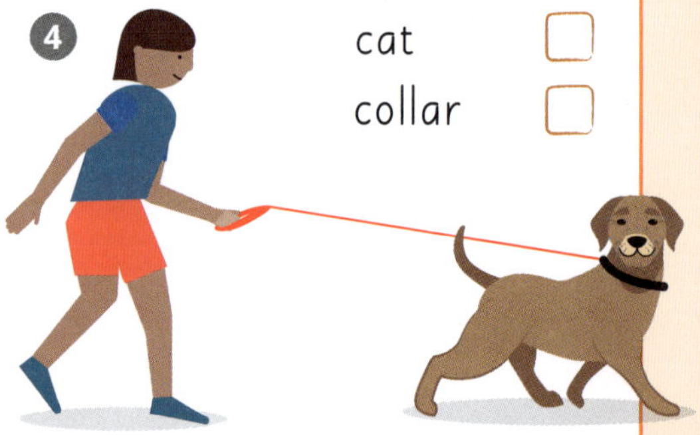

Now listen and repeat.

10.4 Look at the pictures and write the correct words.

| vet | ~~fish~~ | dog | mouse | tortoise | cat |

fish

1 _____

2 _____

3 _____

4 _____

5 _____

Now listen and repeat.

10.5 Listen and tick the correct pictures.

A ☐   B ✔

1   A ☐   B ☐

2   A ☐   B ☐

3   A ☐   B ☐

4   A ☐   B ☐

10.6 Listen to the song and write the correct words in the spaces.

I've got a _**cat**_ ,
she's _____ and _____ .
She likes to run
and play with a ball.

Maria's got a _____ ,
his name is Socks.
He's _____ and _____
and he's in this box.

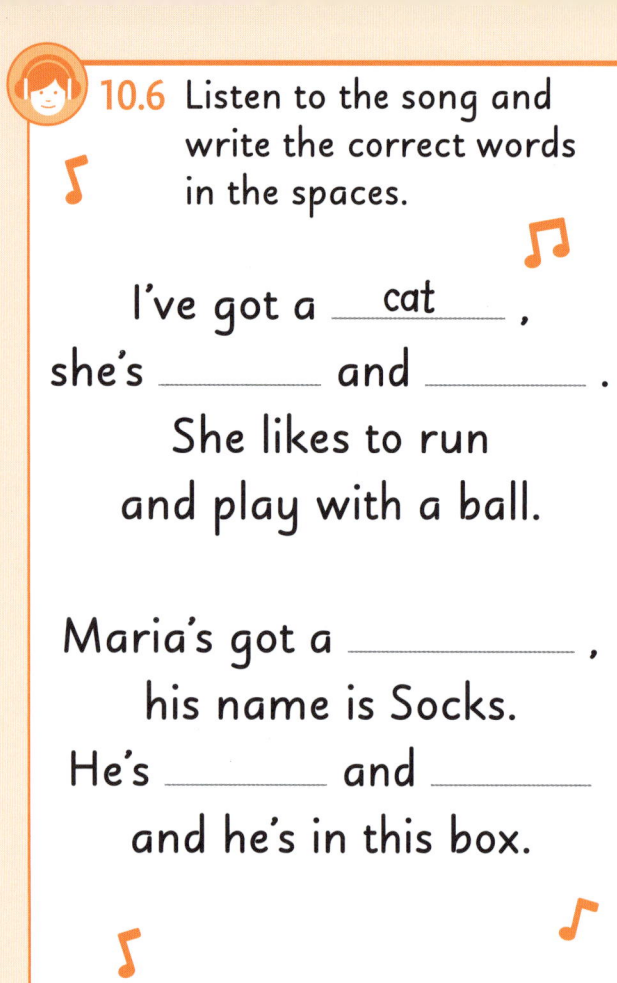

10.7 Match the pictures to the correct words.

Ben's got a rabbit.

1

He's got a mouse.

2

She's got a fish.

3

Sara's got a tortoise.

4

He's got a cat.

5

She's got a cat.

Now listen and repeat.

10.8 Listen and tick the correct pictures.

A ☐   B ✓

① A ☐   B ☐

② A ☐   B ☐

③ A ☐   B ☐

④ A ☐   B ☐

⑤ A ☐   B ☐

10.9 Look at the pictures and tick the correct answers.

Has she got a dog?

Yes, she has. ☐

No, she hasn't. ☑

1 Has he got a cat?

Yes, he has. ☐

No, he hasn't. ☐

2 Has she got a tortoise?

Yes, she has. ☐

No, she hasn't. ☐

3 Has he got a spider?

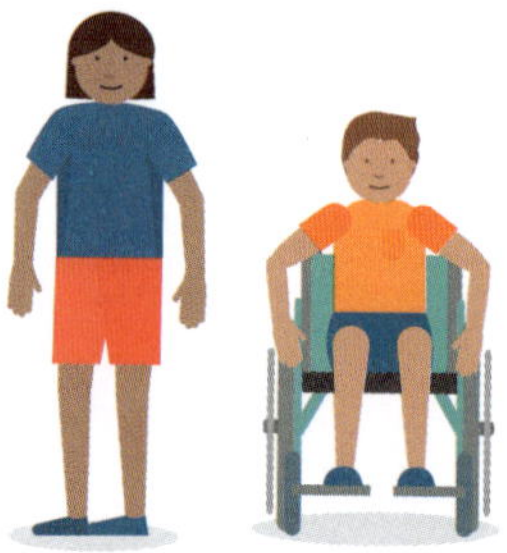

Yes, he has. ☐

No, he hasn't. ☐

Now listen and repeat.

Read the questions and tick the correct pictures.

Which dog is clean?

A ✔ B ☐

❶ Which one is nice?

A ☐ B ☐

❷ Which dog is small?

A ☐ B ☐

❸ Which one is young?

A ☐ B ☐

❹ Which dog is dirty?

A ☐ B ☐

❺ Which one is old?

A ☐ B ☐

Now listen and repeat.

10.11 **There are four sentences. Mark the beginning and end of each one and write them below.**

Which pet is small?

❶ _____

❷ _____

❸ _____

Whichpetissmall? Themouse.Whichoneisscary?Thespider!

Now listen and repeat.

11 My body

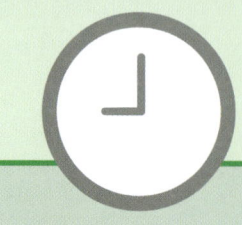

11.1 Listen and write the correct words in the spaces.

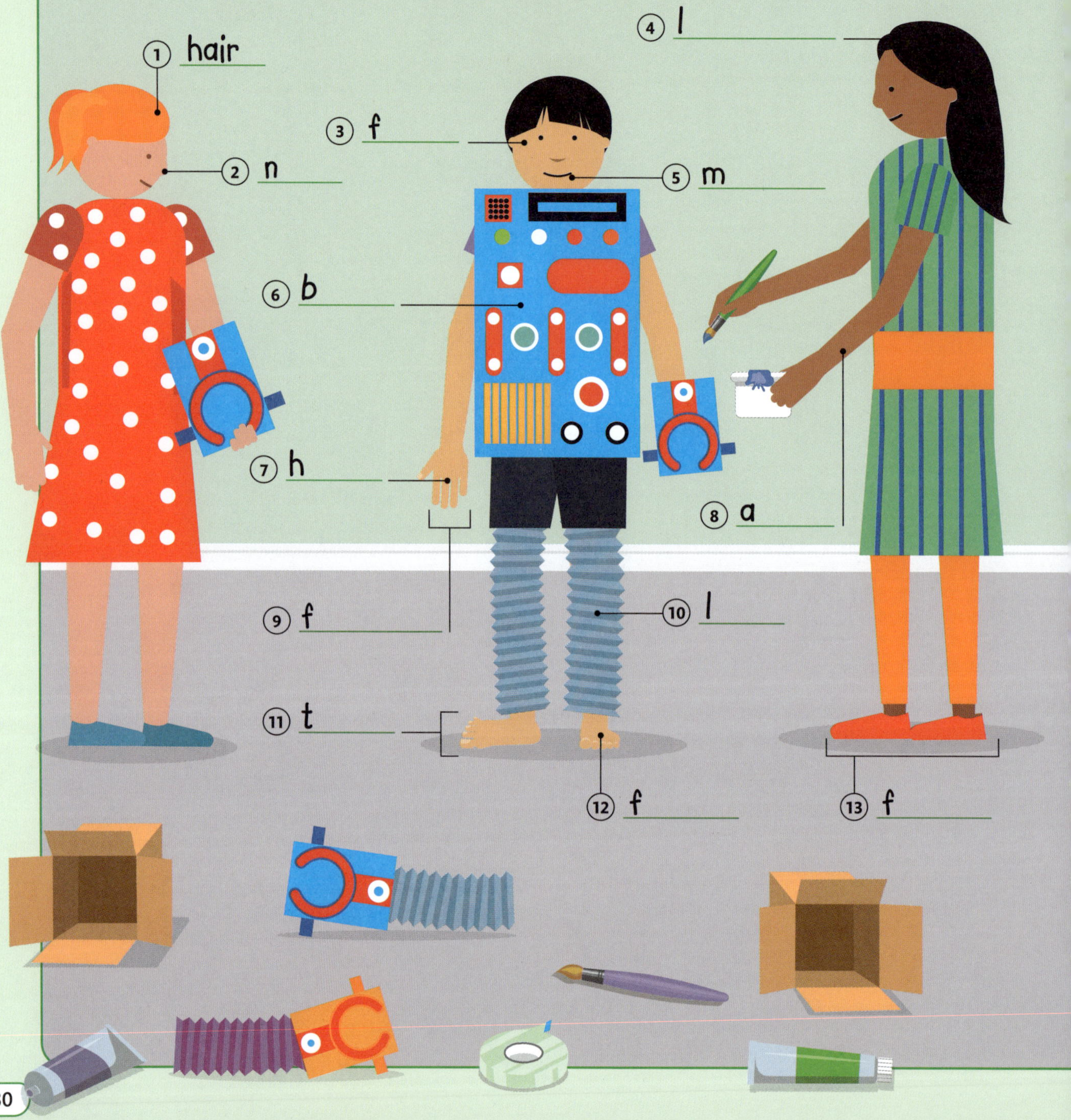

1 hair
2 n
3 f
4 l
5 m
6 b
7 h
8 a
9 f
10 l
11 t
12 f
13 f

body   nose   mouth   face   ~~hair~~   arm

hand   toes   long hair   foot   leg   feet   fingers

head   ear   short hair   teeth   eye

14 h ___

The robot's got red eyes.

15 s ___

16 e ___

17 e ___

18 t ___

11.2 Find and circle the five words in the grid.

teeth   fingers   ~~leg~~   hair   feet   arm

d g f l b x a
t e e t h h r
r (l e g) n a m
j k t k b i f
f i n g e r s

11.3 Match the pictures to the correct words.

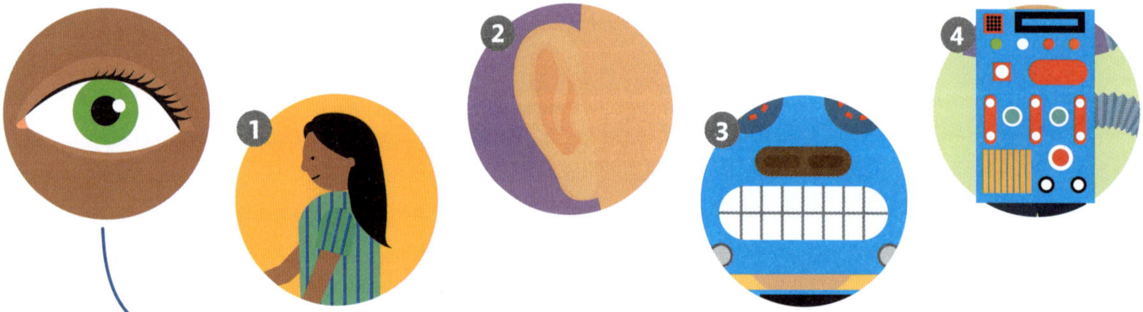

ear   eye   body   long hair   teeth

Now listen and repeat.

11.4 Write the correct words next to the pictures.

t o e s

1. _ _ _ _

2. _ _ _

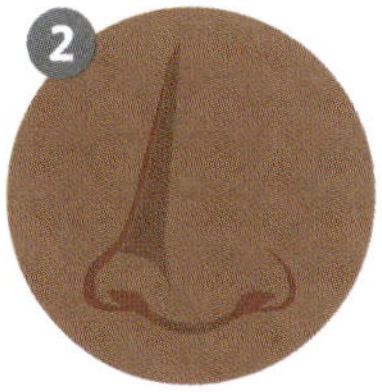

3. _ _ _

4. _ _ _ _

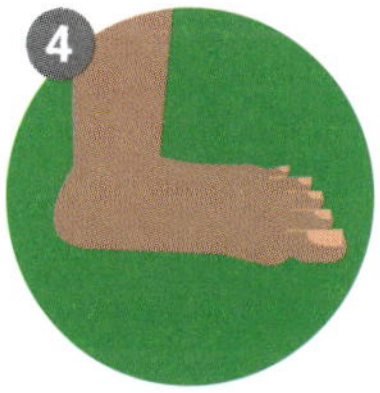

5. _ _ _

Now listen and repeat.

11.5 Listen and tick the correct pictures.

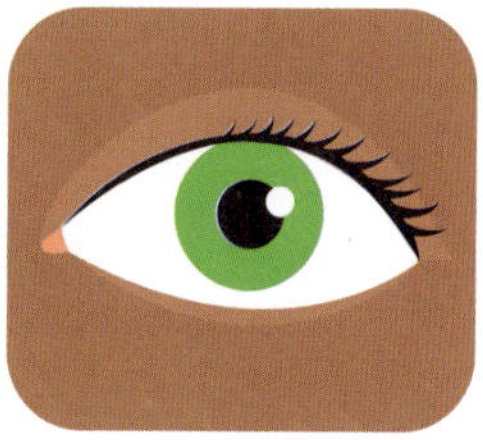

A ☐   B ☑

1.   A ☐   B ☐

2.   A ☐   B ☐

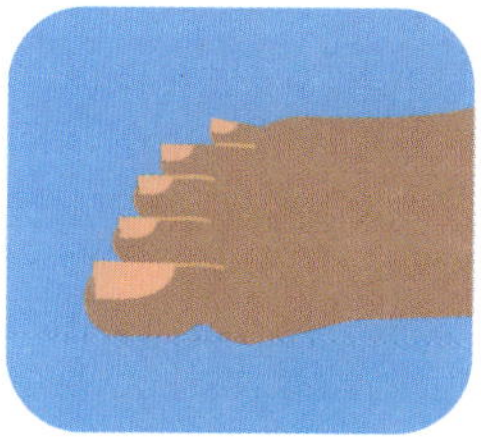

3.   A ☐   B ☐

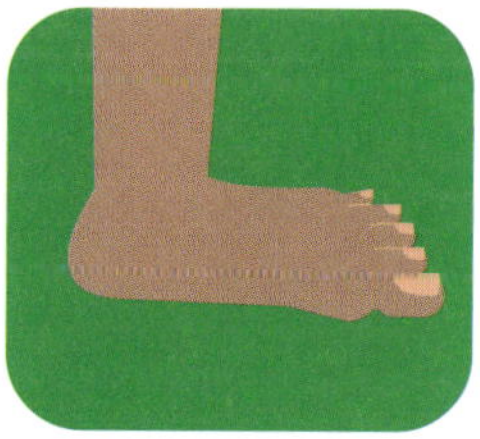

11.6 Look at the picture and write the correct words in the spaces.

legs   purple   ~~ears~~   teeth
hands   yellow   blue

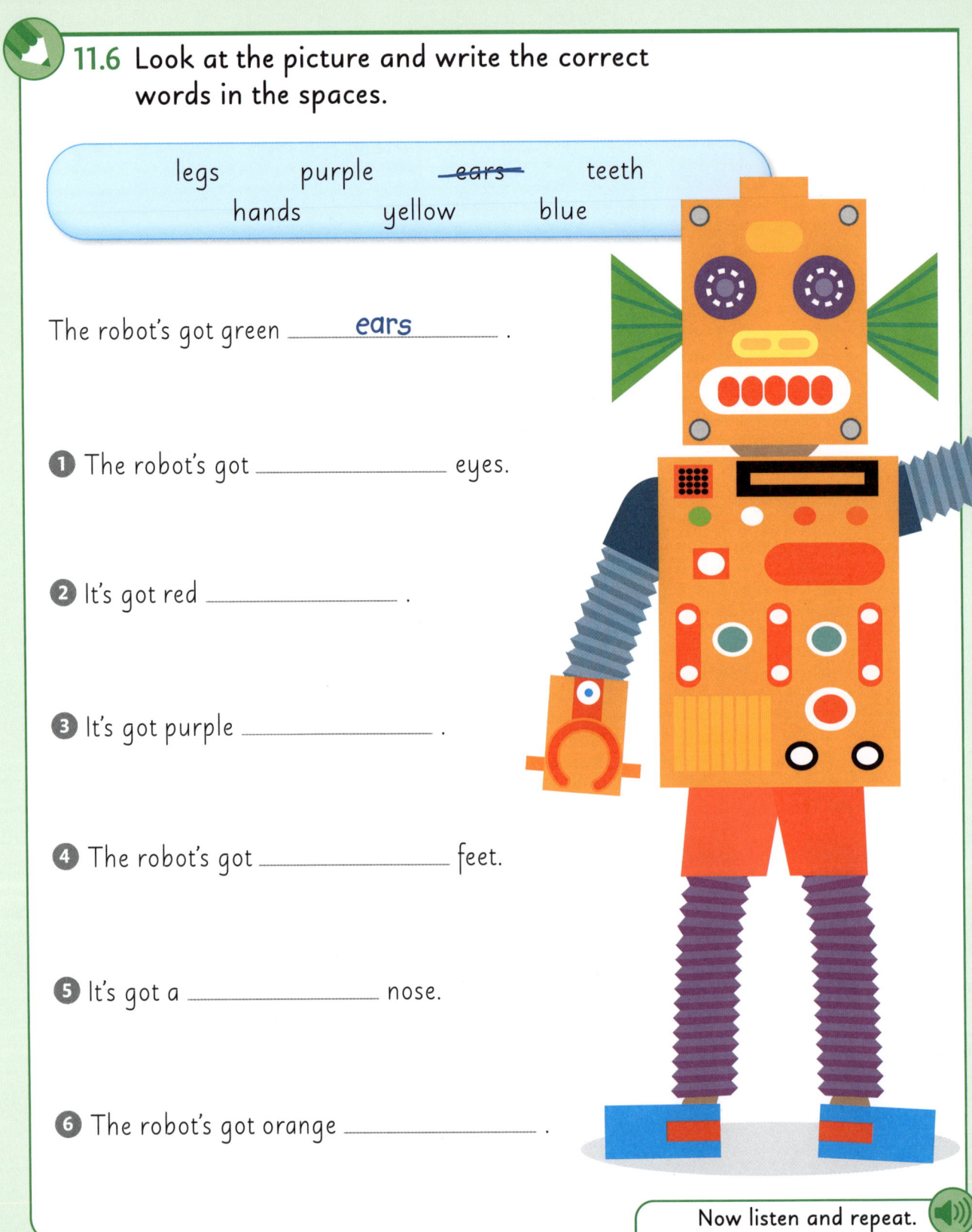

The robot's got green _____ears_____ .

❶ The robot's got _____ eyes.

❷ It's got red _____ .

❸ It's got purple _____ .

❹ The robot's got _____ feet.

❺ It's got a _____ nose.

❻ The robot's got orange _____ .

Now listen and repeat.

84

11.7 Listen and colour in the robot.

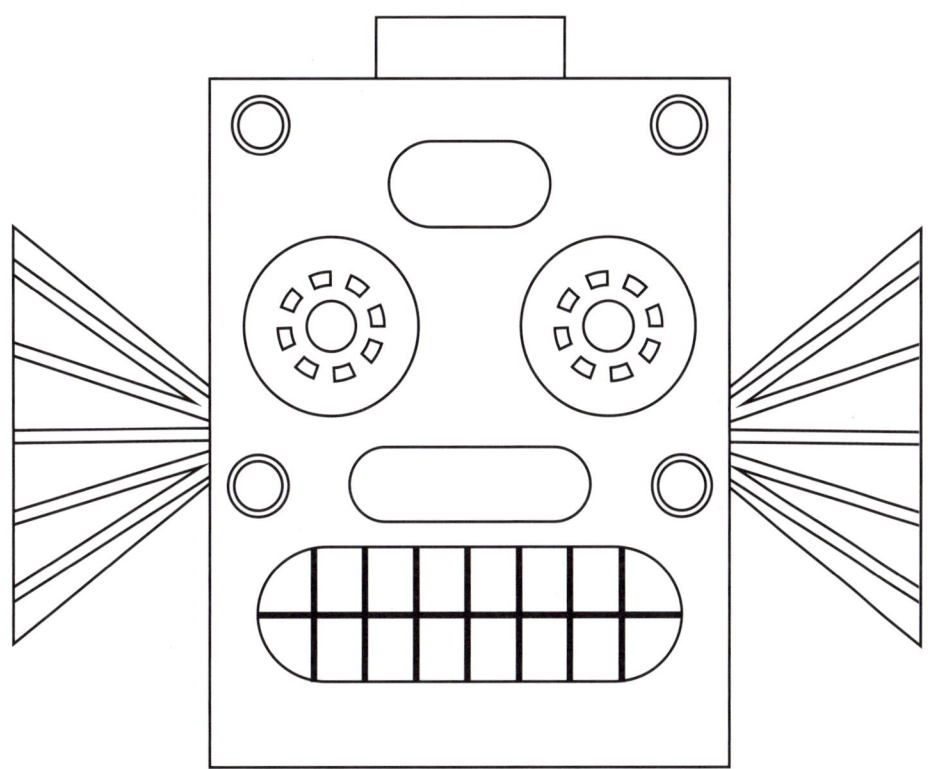

 11.8 Listen and circle the correct answers.

Has the robot got four arms?

(Yes, it has.) / No, it hasn't.

1 Has it got black feet?

Yes, it has. / No, it hasn't.

2 Has it got green eyes?

Yes, it has. / No, it hasn't.

3 Has the robot got orange teeth?

Yes, it has. / No, it hasn't.

4 Has the robot got two legs?

Yes, it has. / No, it hasn't.

5 Has it got purple toes?

Yes, it has. / No, it hasn't.

11.9 Look at the picture and write the correct answers in the spaces.

No, it hasn't.   ~~Yes, it has.~~   Yes, it has.
Yes, it has.   No, it hasn't.   Yes, it has.

Has it got three arms?

Yes, it has.

❶ Has it got purple eyes?

_____

❷ Has it got two legs?

_____

❸ Has it got orange hands?

_____

❹ Has it got blue ears?

_____

❺ Has it got three hands?

_____

Now listen and repeat.

11.10 Match the pictures to the correct words.

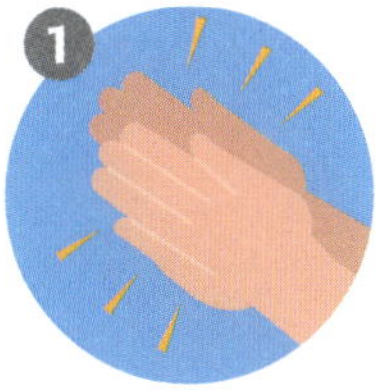

touch   point   wave   clap   move

Now listen and repeat.

11.11 Listen to the song and write the correct words in the spaces.

Clap your hands,
_____ your nose,
_____ your feet,
_____ your toes!

Point one _____ ,
move your head,
_____ your arms,
touch one leg!

12 Our town

12.1 Listen and write the correct words in the spaces.

park aeroplane
train ~~airport~~ lake
bookshop zoo
street boat bike
fire station house
school helicopter
block of flats
shop hospital
bus lorry
motorbike car

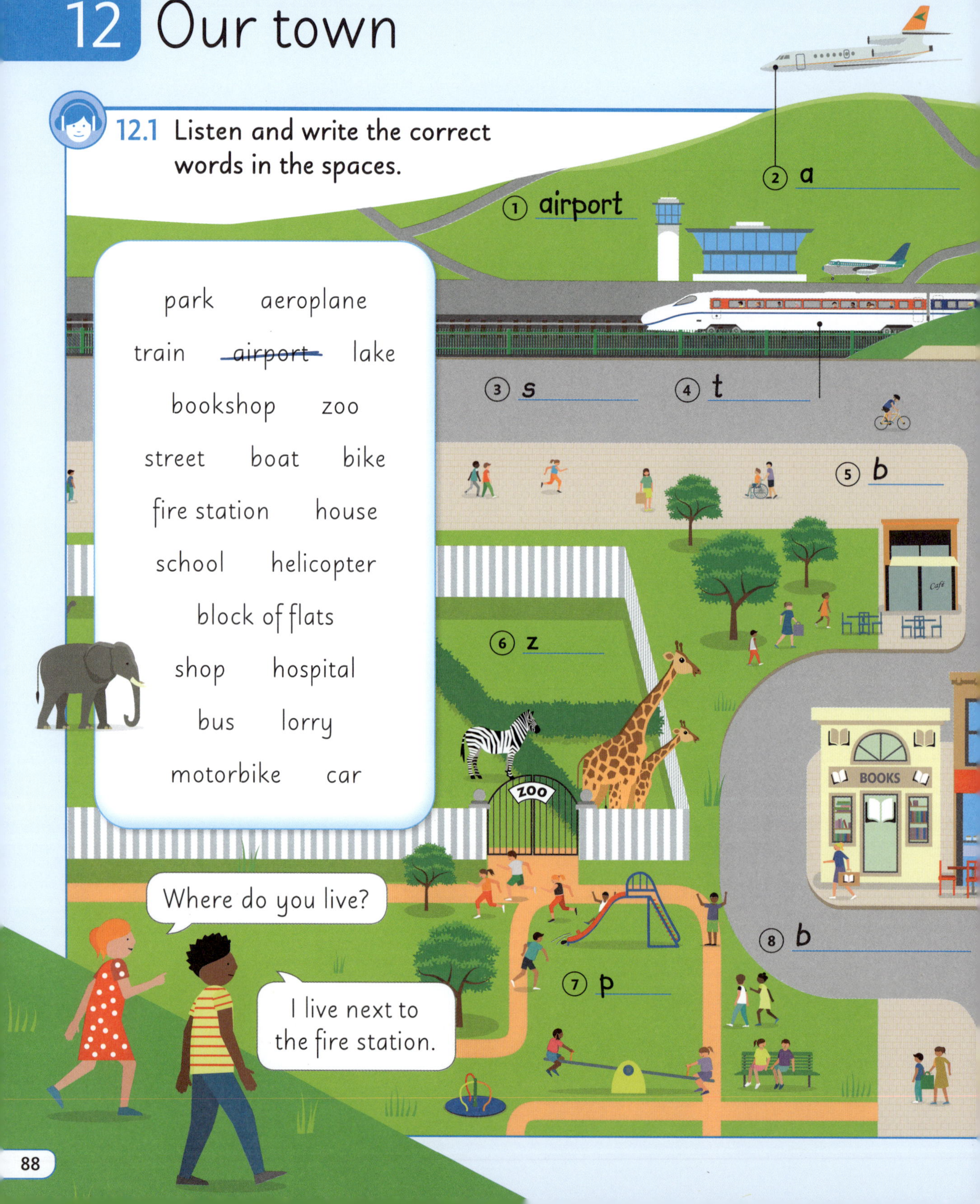

1 airport
2 a
3 s
4 t
5 b
6 z
7 p
8 b
ZOO
BOOKS
Café
Where do you live?
I live next to the fire station.

⑨ l _____

⑩ b _____

⑪ h _____

⑫ s _____

⑬ f _____

⑭ b _____

⑮ h _____

⑯ h _____

⑰ s _____

⑱ l _____

⑲ c _____

⑳ b _____

㉑ m _____

89

12.2 Look at the pictures and circle the correct words.

(zoo) / street

bus / lorry

house / school

bike / helicopter

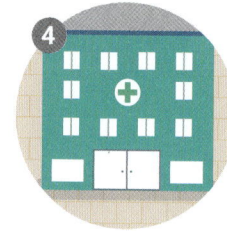

hospital / shop

park / lorry

Now listen and repeat.

12.3 Listen and tick the correct pictures.

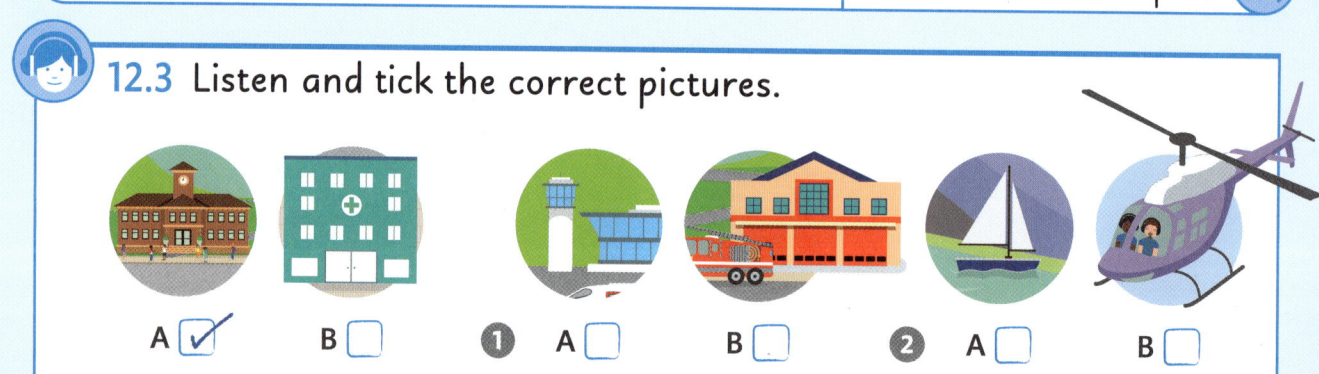

A ✓   B ☐   ① A ☐   B ☐   ② A ☐   B ☐

③ A ☐   B ☐   ④ A ☐   B ☐   ⑤ A ☐   B ☐

12.4 Look at the pictures and write the letters in the correct order.

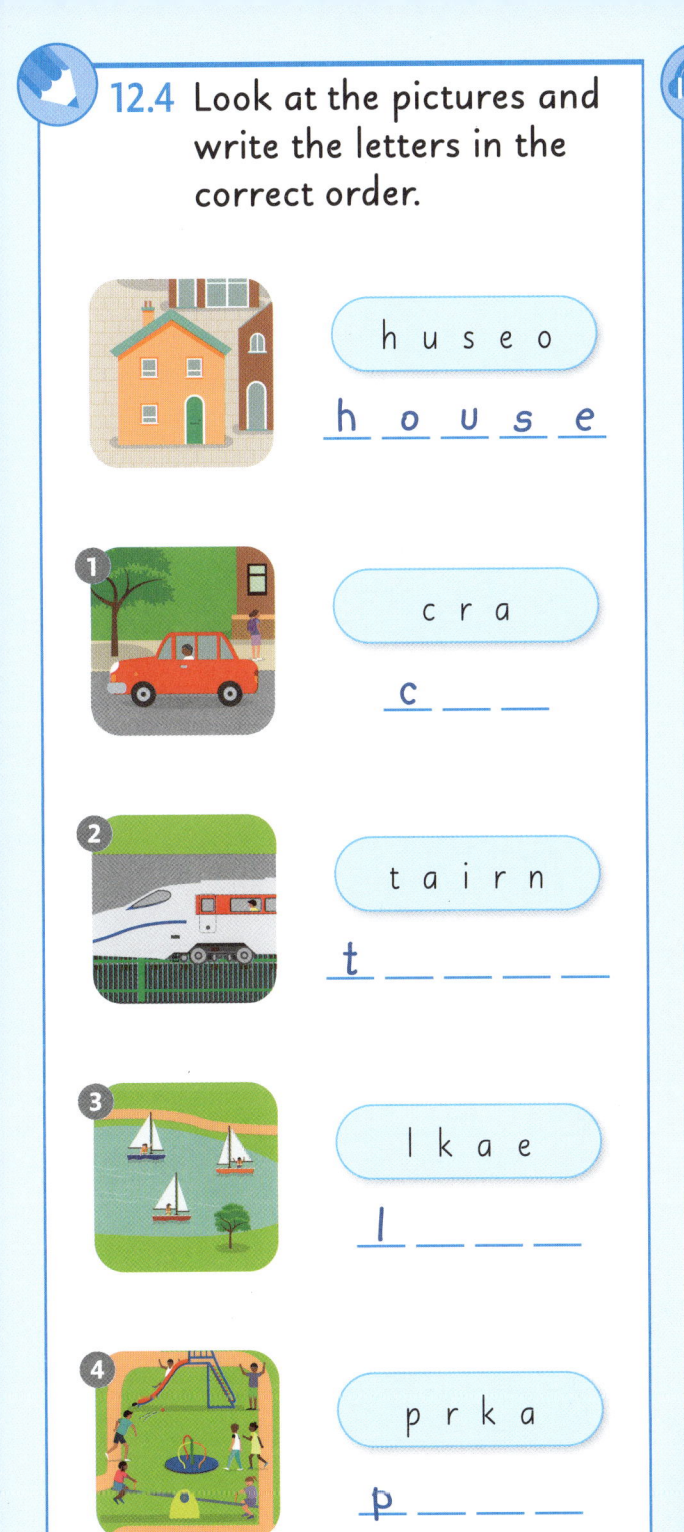

h u s e o
h o u s e

1. c r a
c _ _

2. t a i r n
t _ _ _ _

3. l k a e
l _ _ _

4. p r k a
p _ _ _

Now listen and repeat.

12.5 Listen to the song and write the correct words in the spaces.

This is my town,
there's a __park__
and a _____ .
There's an _____ ,
a _____ , and
a fire station, too.

This is my town,
there are _____ and
a _____ .
This is my town,
I love it, it's cool.

12.6 Look at the pictures and write the correct words in the spaces.

There are   ~~There's~~   There are   There's   There are   There's

There's a lake.

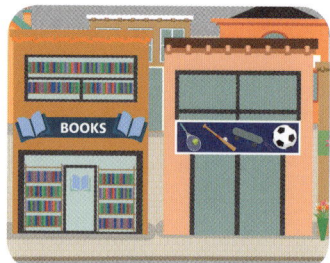

1 _____ two shops.

2 _____ a fire station.

3 _____ a zoo.

4 _____ three houses.

5 _____ four cars.

Now listen and repeat.

12.7 Read the sentences and tick the correct pictures.

There are two motorbikes.

A ☐ B ✓

1 There's a car.

A ☐ B ☐

2 There are four bikes.

A ☐ B ☐

3 There are three boats.

A ☐ B ☐

4 There's a house.

A ☐ B ☐

5 There's a lorry.

A ☐ B ☐

Now listen and repeat. 🔊

12.8 Look at the pictures and tick the correct words.

behind ✓
next to ☐
in front of ☐

1

between ☐
in front of ☐
behind ☐

2

between ☐
next to ☐
in front of ☐

3

behind ☐
between ☐
next to ☐

Now listen and repeat. 🔊

12.9 Look at the picture and write the correct words in the spaces.

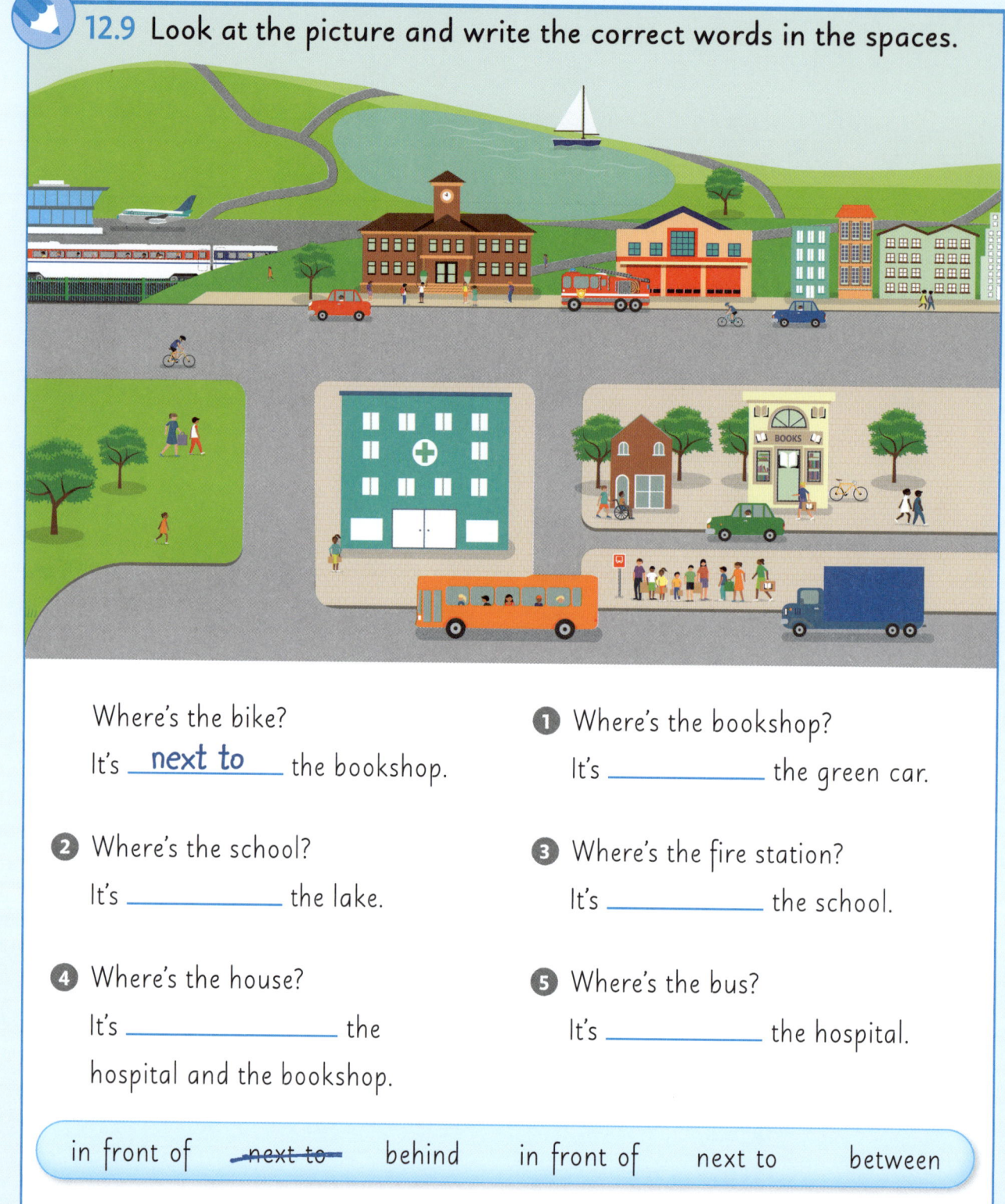

Where's the bike?

It's ___next to___ the bookshop.

1 Where's the bookshop?

It's _____ the green car.

2 Where's the school?

It's _____ the lake.

3 Where's the fire station?

It's _____ the school.

4 Where's the house?

It's _____ the hospital and the bookshop.

5 Where's the bus?

It's _____ the hospital.

in front of   ~~next to~~   behind   in front of   next to   between

Now listen and repeat.

 12.10 **Listen and match the questions to the correct answers.**

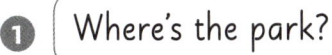

Where do you live?

It's behind the hospital.

1 Where's the park?

It's between the fire station and the shop.

2 Where's the lorry?

It's behind the school.

3 Where's the zoo?

I live in front of the zoo.

4 Where's the lake?

It's between the airport and the block of flats.

5 Where's the school?

It's next to the lake.

I live next to the zoo.

And you?

I live _____

_____

My home

13.1 Listen and write the correct words in the spaces.

plants   bedroom

clock   ~~garden~~

television/TV

sofa   bath   floor

living room   wall

door   window   kitchen

mat   fridge

armchair   dining room

bookcase   hall   chair

mirror   lights   table

bathroom   flowers

② b _____

③ c _____

④ p _____

⑬ l _____

⑭ t _____

⑮ s _____

① __garden__

Where's Sara?

She's in the bedroom.

5 w _____
6 w _____
7 f _____

8 a _____
9 b _____

10 b _____
11 m _____
12 b _____

16 h _____
17 d _____
18 m _____

19 l _____
20 k _____
21 f _____

22 d _____
23 f _____
24 t _____
25 c _____

13.2 Look at the pictures and circle the correct words.

kitchen / (bathroom)

dining room / bathroom

bedroom / living room

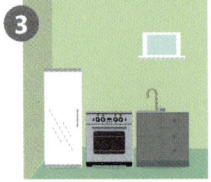

kitchen / living room

bedroom / dining room

kitchen / hall

Now listen and repeat.

 13.3 Match the pictures to the correct words.

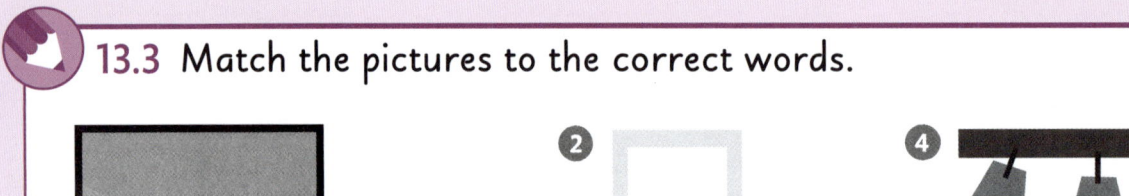

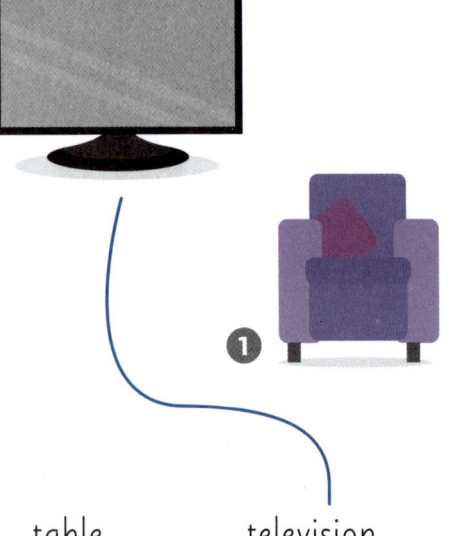

table   television   lights   armchair   window

Now listen and repeat.

13.4 Look at the pictures and tick the correct words.

table ☐
wall ☑
television ☐

1 
sofa ☐
floor ☐
flowers ☐

2 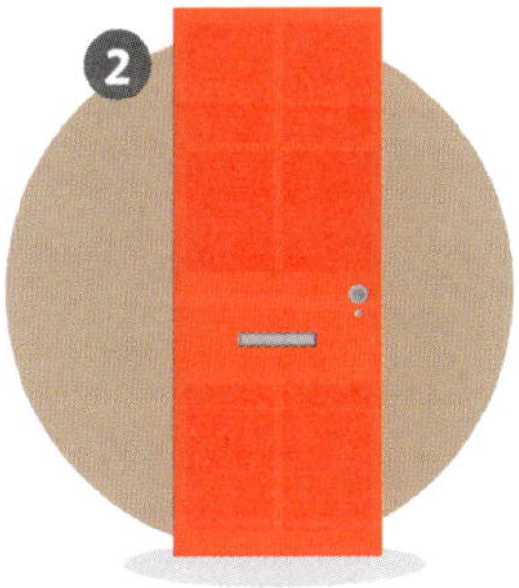
clock ☐
television ☐
door ☐

3 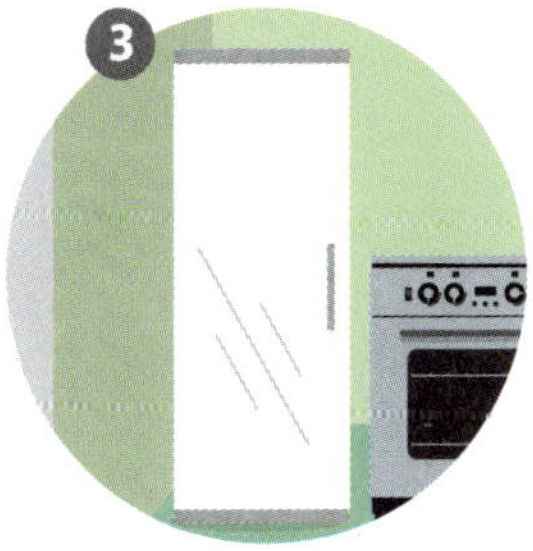
bookcase ☐
fridge ☐
mirror ☐

Now listen and repeat. 🔊

13.5 Look at the pictures and write the correct words in the spaces.

bookcase   ~~door~~
clock   plants   chair

door _____

1 _____

2 _____

3 _____

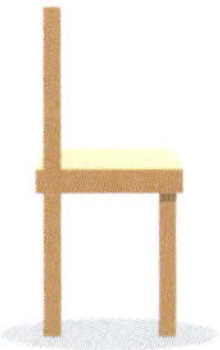

4 _____

Now listen and repeat. 🔊

13.6 Write the correct words under the pictures.

under	~~in~~	on

i n

1 ___ ___

2 ___ ___ ___ ___ ___

Now listen and repeat.

 13.7 Look at the pictures and circle the correct words.

The book is
(on) / under the floor.

The cat is
in / on the bath.

The plants are
on / under the window.

The cat is
on / in the mat.

The bookcase is
under / on the lights.

The flowers are
in / on the table.

Now listen and repeat.

13.8 Listen and tick the correct pictures.

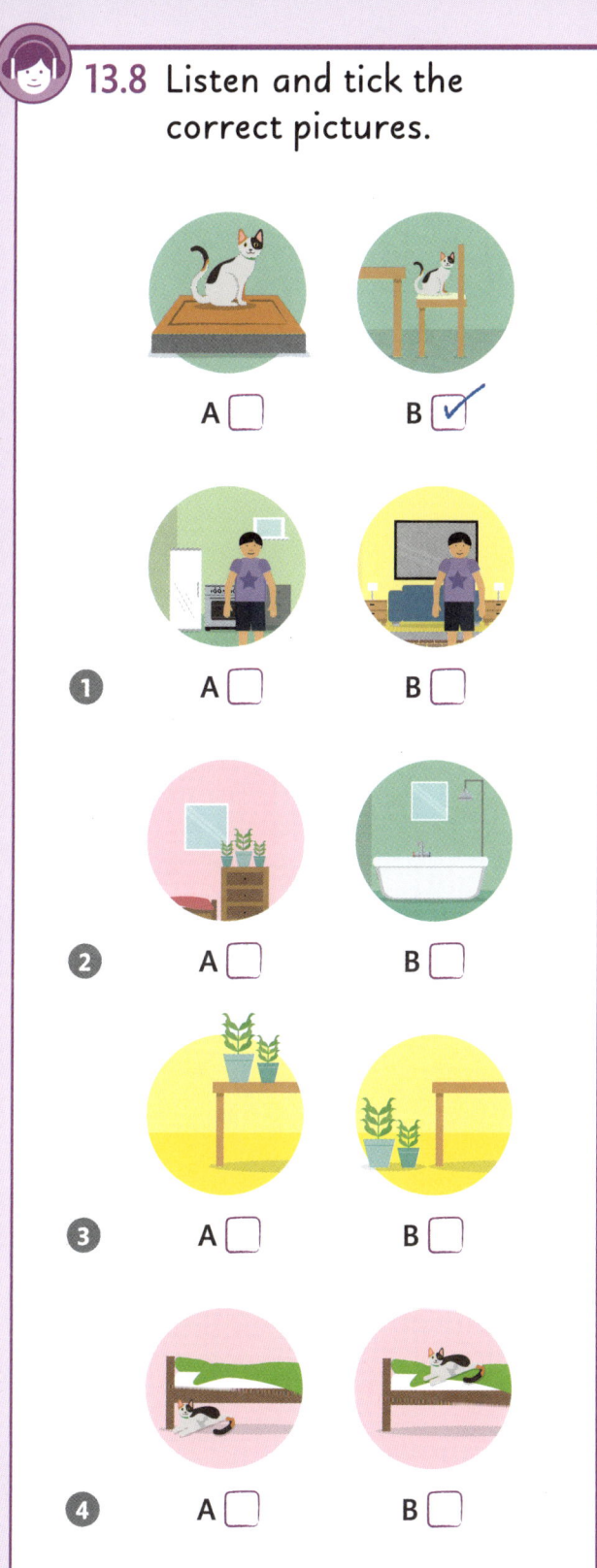

A ☐   B ☑

1 A ☐   B ☐

2 A ☐   B ☐

3 A ☐   B ☐

4 A ☐   B ☐

13.9 Listen to the song and write the correct words in the spaces.

♪   ♫

♫ The TV's __in__
the living room,
the ____ is in the ____ .

Where's the _____ ?
It's ____ my
bedroom ____ .
♪

13.10 Look at the pictures and write the correct answers in the spaces.

Yes, there is.	~~Is there~~	No, there isn't.
No, there isn't.	Yes, there is.	Is there

__Is there__ a TV in the living room?

Yes, there is.

---

① Is there a sofa in the kitchen?

_____

---

② Is there a bookcase in the bedroom?

_____

---

③ Is there a clock in the bathroom?

_____

---

④ Is there a window in the bedroom?

_____

---

⑤ _____ a table in the dining room?

Yes, there is.

Now listen and repeat.

13.11 Look at the picture and write the correct answers in the spaces.

Yes, there are.
No, there aren't.

~~Yes, there are.~~
No, there aren't.

No, there aren't.
Yes, there are.

Are there any plants in the garden?

Yes, there are.

1 Are there any flowers in the kitchen?

_____

2 Are there any windows in
the dining room?

_____

3 Are there any clocks in
the bedroom?

_____

4 Are there any chairs in
the dining room?

_____

5 Are there any armchairs in
the living room?

_____

Now listen and repeat.

14 Review: Where I live

I'm Andy and this is my town.

In my town, there's a hospital and a school.
There are two parks and three shops.

That's my house. I live next to the hospital.

 **14.2 Write about your town then draw your house and town.**

I'm _____ and this is my town.

In my town, there's a _____ and a _____ . There are _____ and _____ .

That's my house. I live _____ the _____ .

15 On the farm

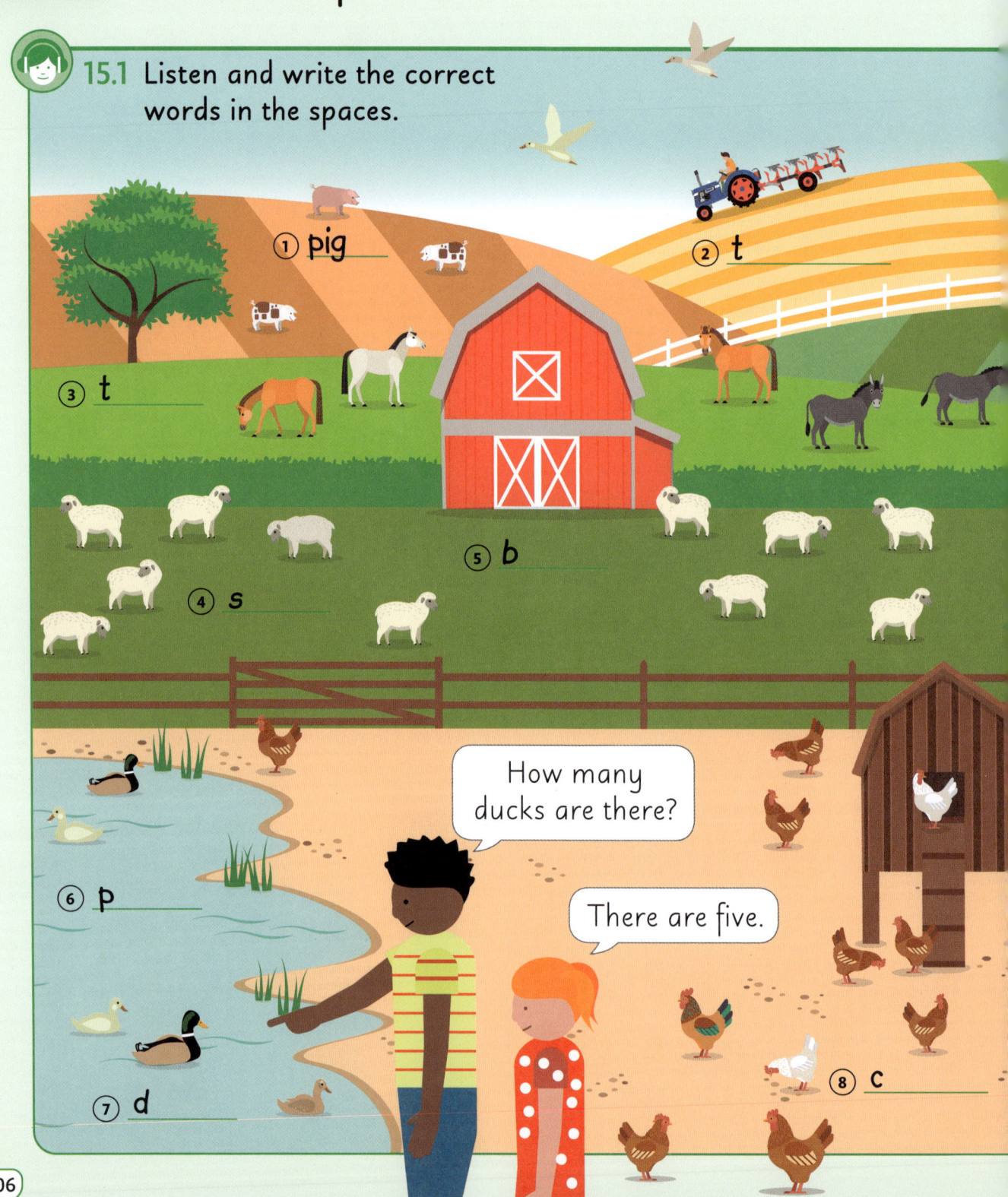

① pig

② t

③ t

④ s

⑤ b

⑥ p

⑦ d

⑧ c

How many ducks are there?

There are five.

106

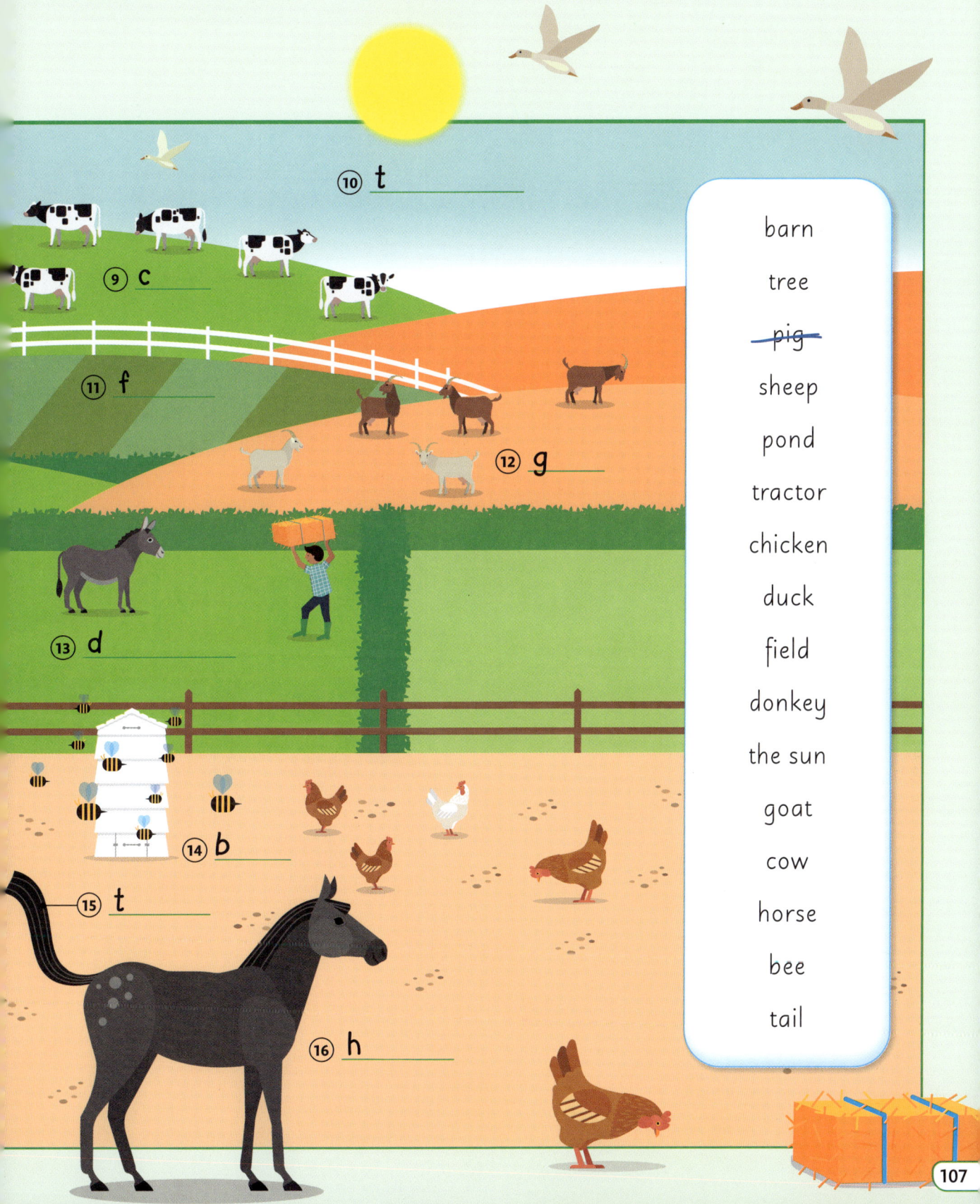

⑩ t _____

⑨ c _____

⑪ f _____

⑫ g _____

⑬ d _____

⑭ b _____

⑮ t _____

⑯ h _____

barn

tree

pig

sheep

pond

tractor

chicken

duck

field

donkey

the sun

goat

cow

horse

bee

tail

 **15.2** Find and circle the five words in the grid.

tail	donkey	~~barn~~
pig	bee	horse

g t d i h b

(b a r n) o e

p i g l r e

r l e w s i

d o n k e y

 15.3 Listen and tick the correct pictures.

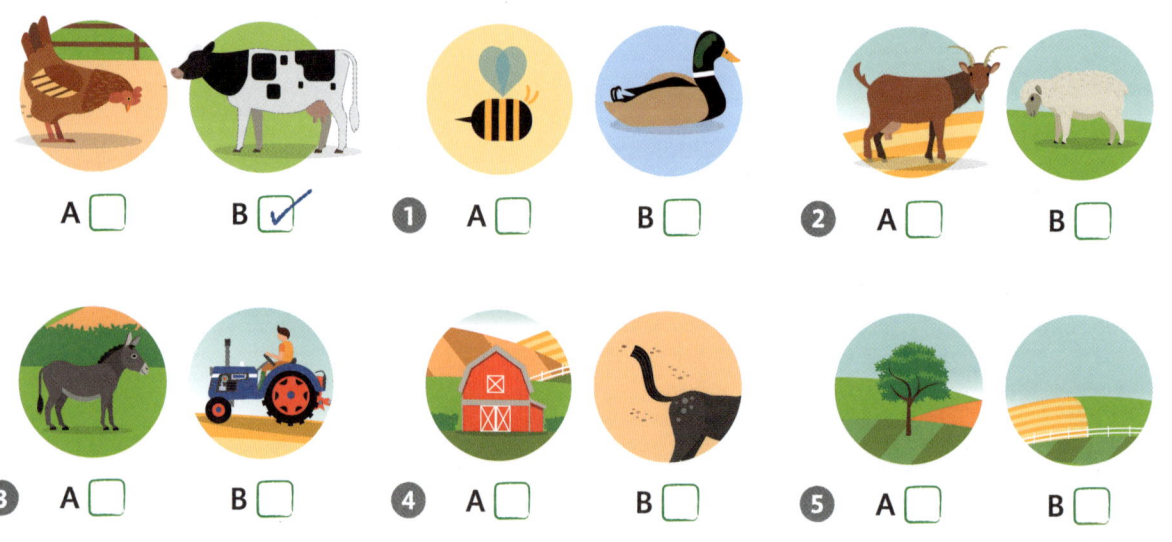

A ☐ B ☑ **1** A ☐ B ☐ **2** A ☐ B ☐

3 A ☐ B ☐ **4** A ☐ B ☐ **5** A ☐ B ☐

15.4 Look at the pictures and circle the correct words.

 (bee) / goat

1.  donkey / pond

2.  sheep / tractor

3. 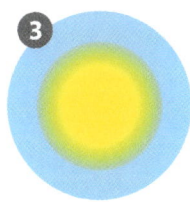 the sun / horse

4.  duck / tail

5.  tree / chicken

Now listen and repeat.

15.5 Look at the pictures and write the correct words in the spaces.

| barn | goat | ~~chicken~~ |
| donkey | field | sheep |

 chicken

1.  _____

2.  _____

3.  _____

4.  _____

5.  _____

Now listen and repeat.

15.6 Look at the picture and match the questions to the correct answers.

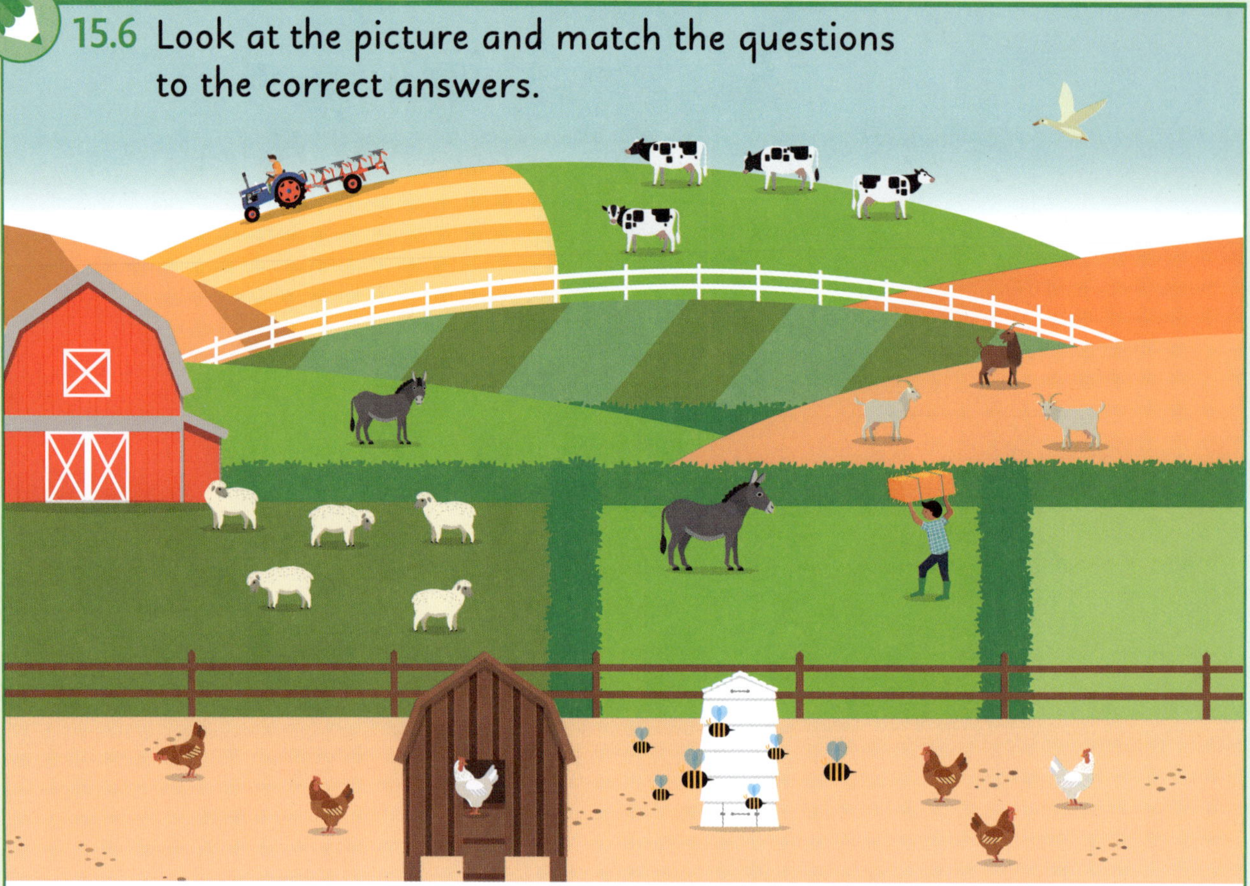

How many barns are there? —— There are five.

1 How many sheep are there? —— There are three.

2 How many cows are there? —— There are six.

3 How many goats are there? —— There's one.

4 How many bees are there? —— There are two.

5 How many chickens are there? —— There are four.

6 How many donkeys are there? —— There are seven.

Now listen and repeat.

15.7 Look at the pictures and circle the correct words.

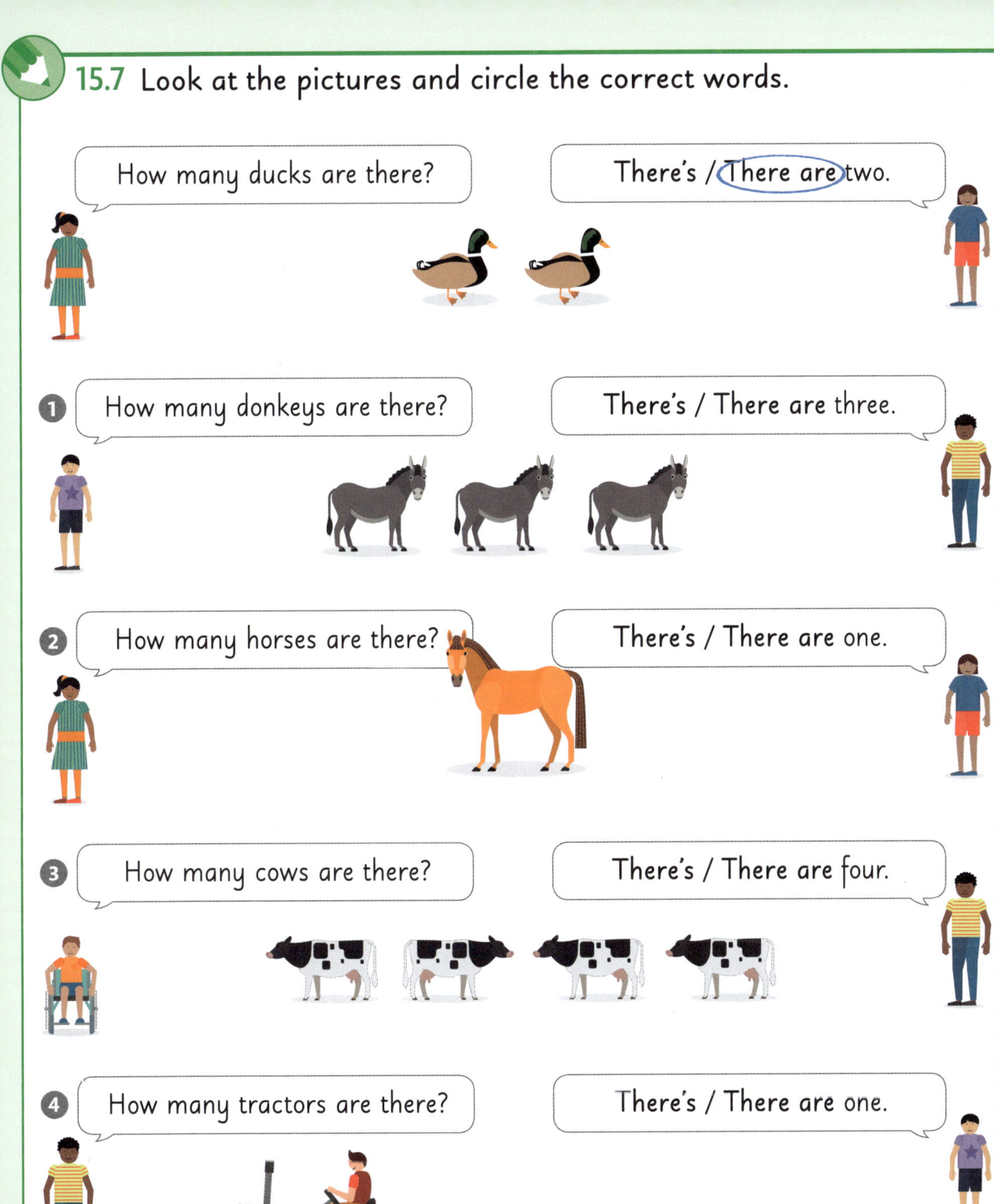

How many ducks are there?

There's / There are two.

1 How many donkeys are there?

There's / There are three.

2 How many horses are there?

There's / There are one.

3 How many cows are there?

There's / There are four.

4 How many tractors are there?

There's / There are one.

Now listen and repeat.

15.8 Look at the pictures and write the correct words in the spaces.

behind · in · next to · in front of

Where are the cows?

They're _____ in _____ the field.

1 Where's the horse?

It's _____ the tree.

2 Where's the donkey?

It's _____ the pond.

3 Where are the goats?

They're _____ the barn.

Now listen and repeat.

15.9 Listen to the song and write the correct words in the spaces.

Where are the ___ducks___ ?
They're on the _____ !

Where are the _____ ?
They're _____ the field!

Where are the _____ ?
They're in the _____ !

_____ are the animals?
They're _____ my farm!

15.10 Look at the pictures and tick the correct sentences.

The donkey's in the field. ✓
The donkeys are in the field. ☐

The duck's on the pond. ☐
The ducks are on the pond. ☐

The sheep's in front of the barn. ☐
The sheep are in front of the barn. ☐

The horse is under the tree. ☐
The horses are under the tree. ☐

Now listen and repeat.

16 Sports

16.1 Listen and write the correct words in the spaces.

① basketball

② b _____

③ f _____

④ t _____

basketball baseball

table tennis ice hockey

tennis football

swimming badminton

⑤ b _____

⑥ s _____

⑦ t _____

⑧ i _____

16.2 Write the correct words under the pictures.

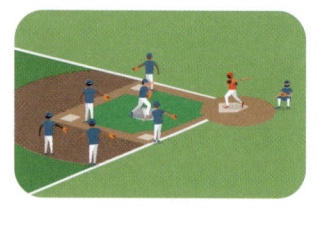

<u>b a s e b a l l</u>

<u>b _ _ _ _ _ _ _ _</u>

<u>t _ _ _ _ _ _</u>

<u>s _ _ _ _ _ _ _</u>

Now listen and repeat.

16.3 Listen and tick the correct pictures.

A ☐   B ✓

① A ☐   B ☐

② A ☐   B ☐

③ A ☐   B ☐

④ A ☐   B ☐

⑤ A ☐   B ☐

16.4 Look at the pictures and write the correct words in the spaces.

swim   play tennis   ~~run~~   bounce   throw
catch   kick   play ice hockey   hit   jump

run

1 j _____

2 s _____

3 p _____

4 p _____

5 c _____

6 b _____

7 k _____

8 t _____

9 h _____

Now listen and repeat.

16.5 Look at the pictures and circle the correct words.

(run) / hit

① swim / run

② jump / kick

③ catch / bounce

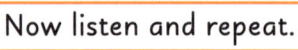

④ throw / hit

Now listen and repeat.

16.6 Read the words and tick the correct pictures.

jump

A ☐   B ✓

① play tennis

A ☐   B ☐

② run

A ☐   B ☐

③ bounce

A ☐   B ☐

④ play basketball

A ☐   B ☐

⑤ throw

A ☐   B ☐

Now listen and repeat.

16.7 Look at the pictures and write the correct words in the spaces.

> jump   catch   ~~kick~~
> throw   bounce

kick

1. _____

2. _____

3. _____

4. _____

Now listen and repeat.

16.8 Match the pictures to the correct words.

play football

1. play baseball

2. play tennis

3. play badminton

4. play ice hockey

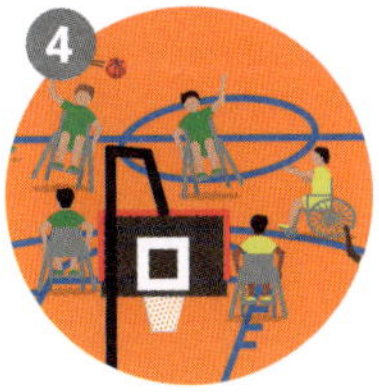

5. play basketball

Now listen and repeat.

16.9 Listen and write the correct words in the spaces.

| can't | can | ~~can't~~ | can | can't | can | can't |

I _____can't_____ play table tennis.

1 I _____ play tennis.

2 I _____ play baseball.

3 I _____ play ice hockey.

4 I _____ play basketball.

5 I _____ play badminton.

6 I _____ play football.

16.10 Listen and tick the correct answers.

Can you bounce a ball?

Yes, I can. ✓

No, I can't. ☐

1 Can you swim?

Yes, I can. ☐

No, I can't. ☐

2 Can you play basketball?

Yes, I can. ☐

No, I can't. ☐

3 Can you throw a ball?

Yes, I can. ☐

No, I can't. ☐

4 Can you play football?

Yes, I can. ☐

No, I can't. ☐

16.11 Look at the pictures and write the correct words in the spaces.

she can   Can she   ~~he can't~~

Can he   she can't   he can

Can he play tennis?

No, _he can't_ .

1 Can he catch a ball?

Yes, _____ .

2 _____ run?

Yes, she can.

3 Can she play football?

No, _____ .

4 Can she swim?

Yes, _____ .

5 _____ play baseball?

No, he can't.

Now listen and repeat.

122

Can Max swim? ———————————— Yes, he can.

1 Can she play table tennis?   No, she can't.

2 Can Maria play badminton?   Yes, she can.

3 Can he play ice hockey? ———————— No, he can't.

16.13 There are four sentences. Mark the beginning
and end of each one and write them below.

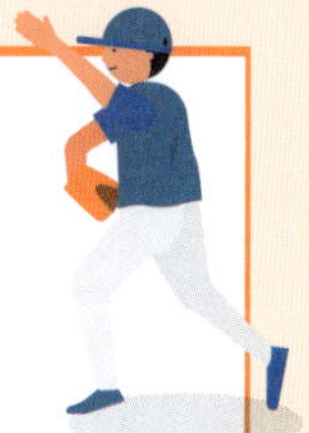

<u>Can she play baseball?</u>

1 _____

2 _____

3 _____

Cansheplaybaseball?|Yes,shecan.Canheswim?No,hecan't.

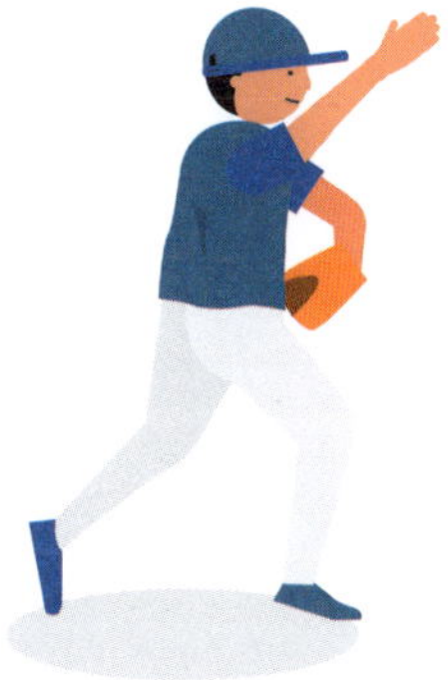

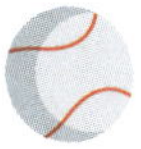

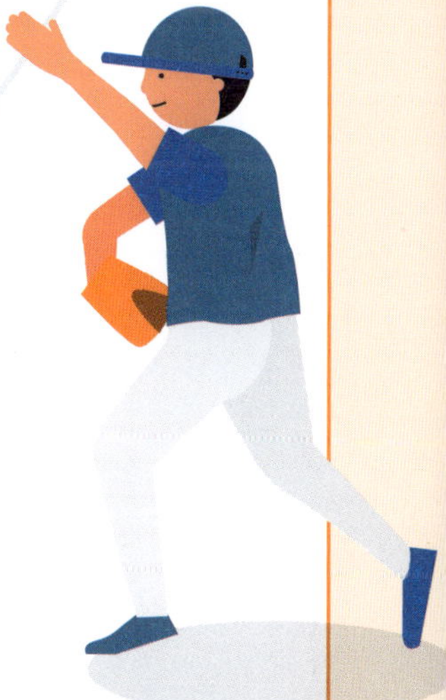

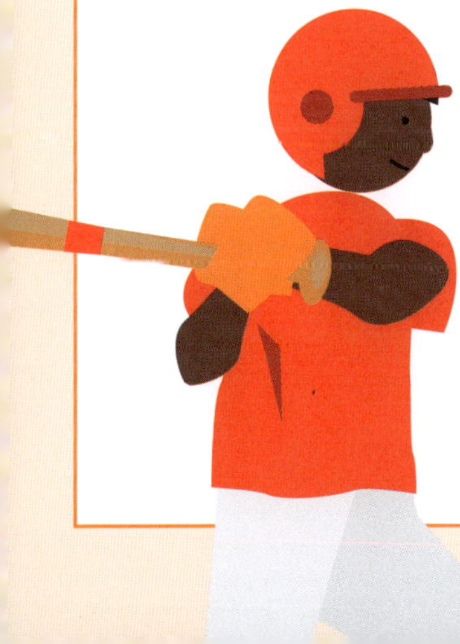

Now listen and repeat.

17 At the food market

① grapes

② l

③ b

④ l   ⑤ k   ⑥ m   ⑦ p   ⑧ t

⑩ a   ⑪ p   ⑫ o   ⑬ w   ⑭ c

Can I have some pears, please?

Here you are.

⑲ f

⑰ m _____

⑱ f _____

○ o _____

⑮ c _____

⑯ p _____

⑳ v _____

oranges   kiwis   lemons   limes

~~grapes~~   tomatoes   mangoes   pears

pineapples   bananas   meat   coconuts

onions   fruit   watermelons   potatoes

vegetables   carrots   fish   apples

17.2 Look at the pictures and write the letters in the correct order.

o i n s n o

o n i o n s

k w i s i

1 k _ _ _ _ _

p r a e s

2 p _ _ _ _ _

a p l p s e

3 a _ _ _ _ _

f u t r i

4 f _ _ _ _

g p r a e s

5 g _ _ _ _ _

l m e s i

6 l _ _ _ _

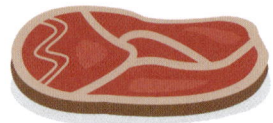

m t a e

7 m _ _ _

l m e n s o

8 l _ _ _ _ _

Now listen and repeat.

17.3 Match the pictures to the correct words.

①  ②  ③  ④

carrots   mangoes   coconuts   watermelons   vegetables

Now listen and repeat.

17.4 Listen to the song and write the correct words in the spaces.
17.5 Colour in the three foods that you heard in the song.

Apples and oranges,
_____ and _____, too.
Here are nice _____,
and meat and _____ for you.

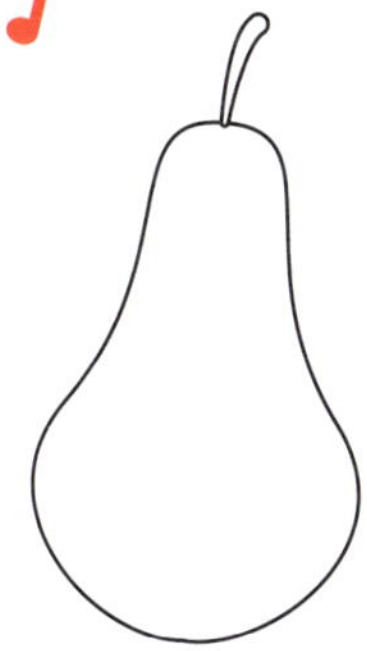

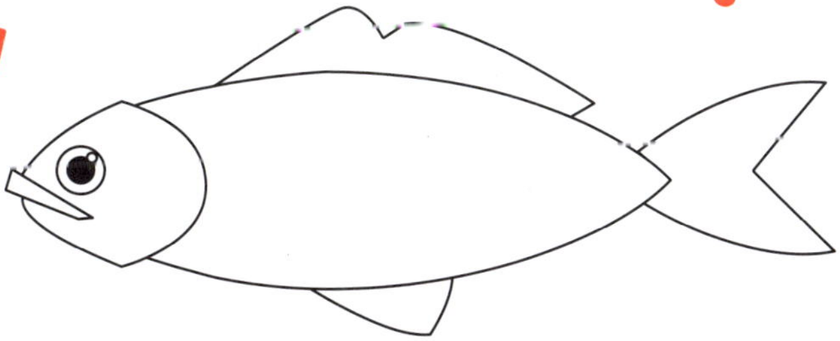

17.6 Look at the pictures and write the correct words in the spaces.

| or | ~~don't like~~ | and | like | and | or |

I **don't like** pears or oranges.

1 I like tomatoes _____ carrots.

2 I don't like potatoes _____ onions.

3 I _____ lemons and limes.

4 I don't like apples _____ coconuts.

5 I like mangoes _____ watermelons.

Now listen and repeat.

Do you like pineapples?

Yes, I do. ✔

No, I don't. ☐

1 Do you like potatoes?

Yes, I do. ☐

No, I don't. ☐

2 Do you like grapes?

Yes, I do. ☐

No, I don't. ☐

3 Do you like meat?

Yes, I do. ☐

No, I don't. ☐

4 Do you like bananas?

Yes, I do. ☐

No, I don't. ☐

17.8 Look at the pictures and circle the correct words.

Can I have **an** / **some** apples, please?

1 Can I have **a** / **some** onions, please?

2 Can I have **a** / **some** lemon, please?

3 Can I have **a** / **some** pears, please?

4 Can I have **an** / **some** orange, please?

5 Can I have **a** / **some** carrots, please?

Now listen and repeat.

17.9 Read the questions and tick the correct pictures.

Can I have some tomatoes, please?

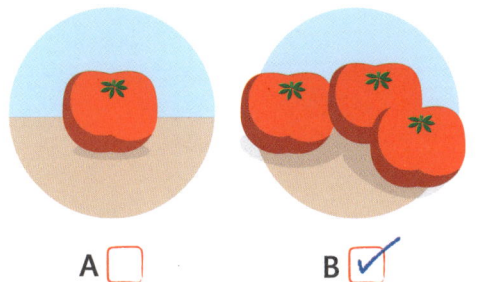

A ☐   B ☑

1 Can I have a potato, please?

A ☐   B ☐

2 Can I have some coconuts, please?

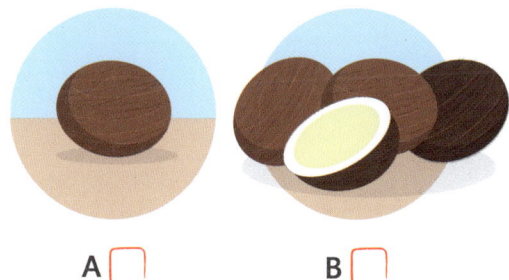

A ☐   B ☐

3 Can I have an apple, please?

A ☐   B ☐

4 Can I have a kiwi, please?

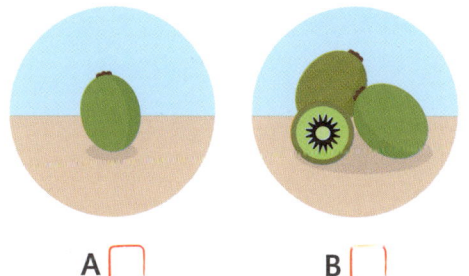

A ☐   B ☐

5 Can I have some bananas, please?

A ☐   B ☐

Now listen and repeat.

18.1 Listen and write the correct words in the spaces.

ball

action figure

~~alien~~

teddy bear

monster

doll

puppet

car

board game

train

rocket

video game

the moon

balloons

stars

robot

① alien

② p _____

③ t _____

④ a _____

⑤ b _____

⑥ d _____

⑦ m _____

⑧ c _____

TOYS

9 r _____ 10 t _____

11 s _____

13 b _____

12 r _____

15 y _____

16 b _____

It's Ben's birthday.

14 t _____

Let's give him a robot.

TOYS

18.2 Listen and tick the correct pictures.

A ☐   B ☑

① A ☐   B ☐

② A ☐   B ☐

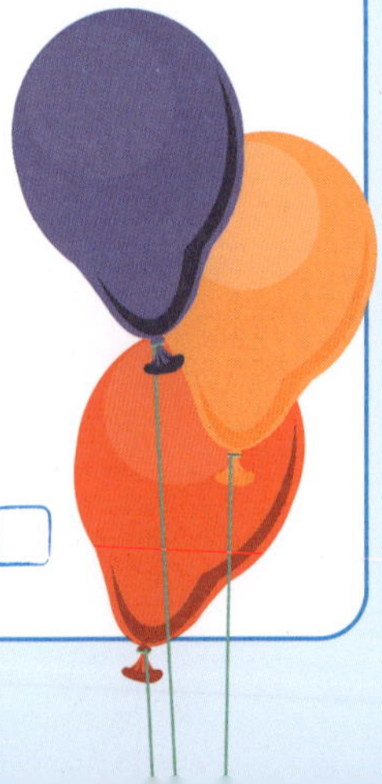

③ A ☐   B ☐

18.3 Look at the pictures and write the letters in the correct order.

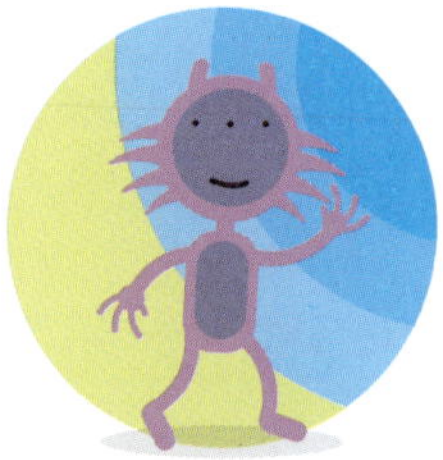

a i n l e
a l i e n

① d l o l
d _ _ _ _

② b l l a
b _ _ _ _

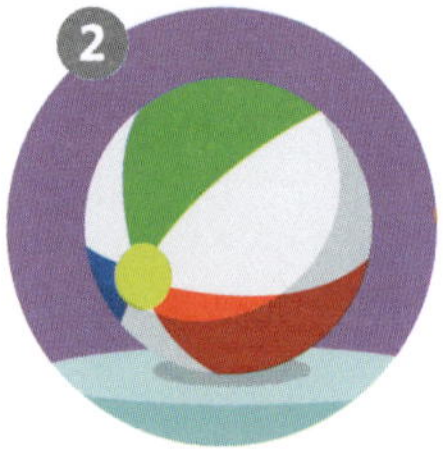

③ t n r a i
t _ _ _ _ _

④ s r t s a
s _ _ _ _ _

Now listen and repeat.

18.4 Look at the pictures and circle the correct words.

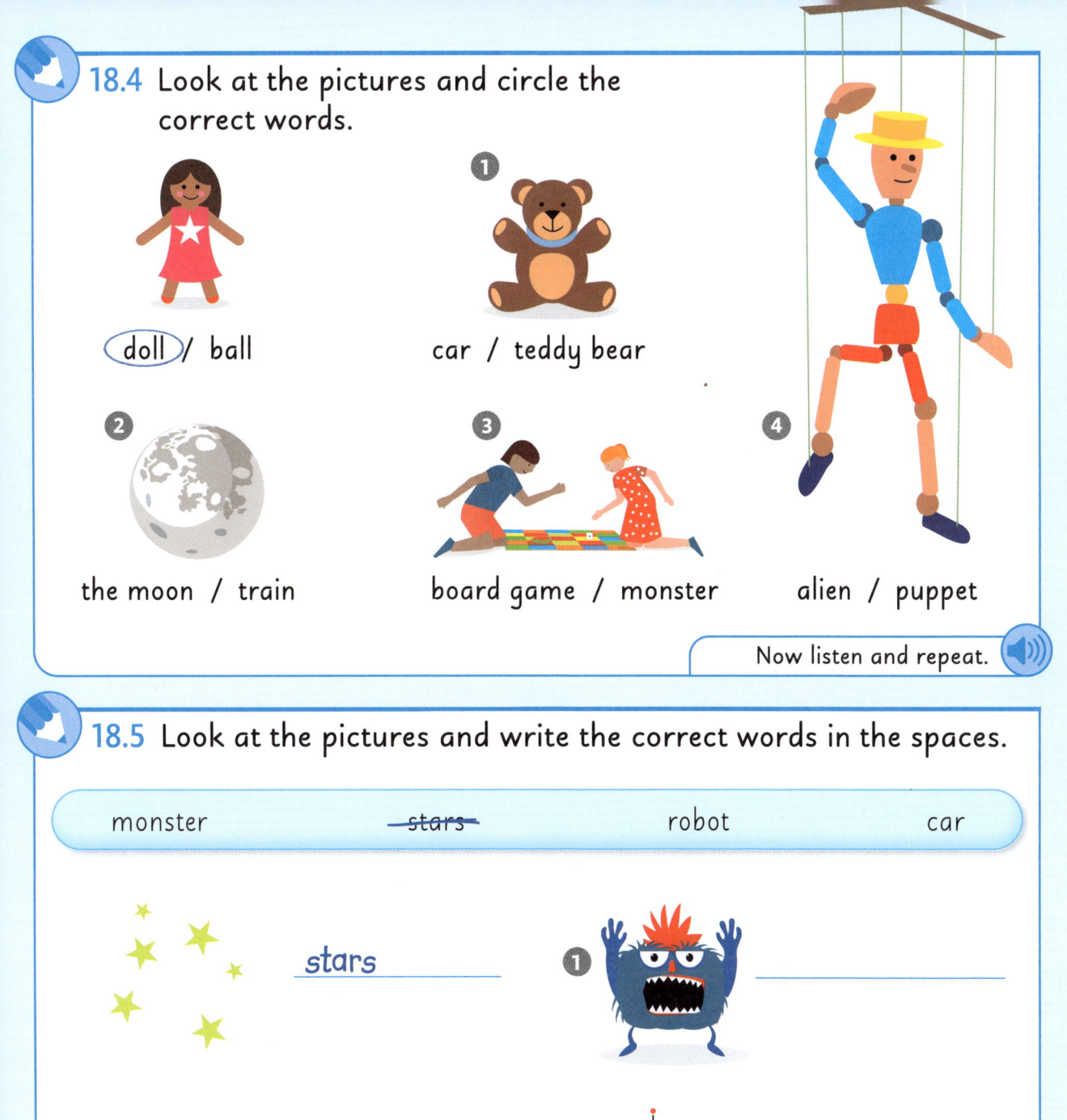

doll / ball

1 car / teddy bear

2 the moon / train

3 board game / monster

4 alien / puppet

Now listen and repeat.

18.5 Look at the pictures and write the correct words in the spaces.

monster   stars   robot   car

stars

1 _____

2 _____

3 _____

Now listen and repeat.

18.6 Listen and write the correct answers in the spaces.

No, she doesn't.   ~~Yes, he does.~~

Yes, she does.   No, he doesn't.

Does he like aliens?

Yes, he does.

1 Does she like board games?

2 Does she like video games?

3 Does he like robots?

18.7 Look at the pictures and circle the correct words.

Ben (likes) / doesn't like trains.

1 She **likes / doesn't like** puppets.

2 Maria **likes / doesn't like** aliens.

3 He **likes / doesn't like** cars.

4 Sara **likes / doesn't like** rockets.

5 Max **likes / doesn't like** monsters.

6 He **likes / doesn't like** dolls.

7 She **likes / doesn't like** balloons.

Now listen and repeat.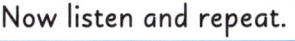

 **18.8 Listen and tick the correct answers.**

I love cars!

Me too! ☑

I don't. ☐

1 I love teddy bears!

Me too! ☐

I don't. ☐

2 I love video games!

Me too! ☐

I don't. ☐

3 I love action figures!

Me too! ☐

I don't. ☐

18.9 Listen to the song and write the correct words in the spaces.

18.10 Colour in the three toys that you heard in the song.

Maria likes ___dolls___ ,
but she doesn't like _____ .
Andy likes _____ ,
but he doesn't like _____ .
I like _____ and video games,
and my favourite toy
is my _____ !

19 Our hobbies

Listen and write the correct words in the spaces.

① <u>ride a bike</u>

② w _____

Word box:
- draw pictures
- ~~ride a bike~~
- paint
- skateboard
- watch football
- play the guitar
- read
- take photos
- play the piano
- dance
- sing

③ s _____

④ d _____

⑤ p _____

I enjoy painting.

Me too. It's fun!

⑥ r _____

⑦ s _____

⑧ d _____

⑨ p _____

⑩ p _____

⑪ t _____

19.2 Read the words and tick the correct pictures.

play the guitar

A ✔   B ☐

1 read

A ☐   B ☐

2 draw pictures

A ☐   B ☐

3 dance

A ☐   B ☐

4 take photos

A ☐   B ☐

5 skateboard

A ☐   B ☐

Now listen and repeat.

19.3 Look at the pictures and circle the correct words.

read / (ride a bike)

1 dance / skateboard

2 play the piano / read

3 sing / paint

4 watch football / sing

Now listen and repeat.

19.4 Match the pictures to the correct words.

ride a bike   play the piano   draw pictures   take photos   play the guitar

Now listen and repeat.

19.5 Look at the pictures and write the letters in the correct order.

d n e c a

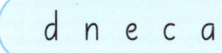
d a n c e

p n t a i

1 p _ _ _ _

r d e a

2 r _ _ _

s g n i

3 s _ _ _

Now listen and repeat.

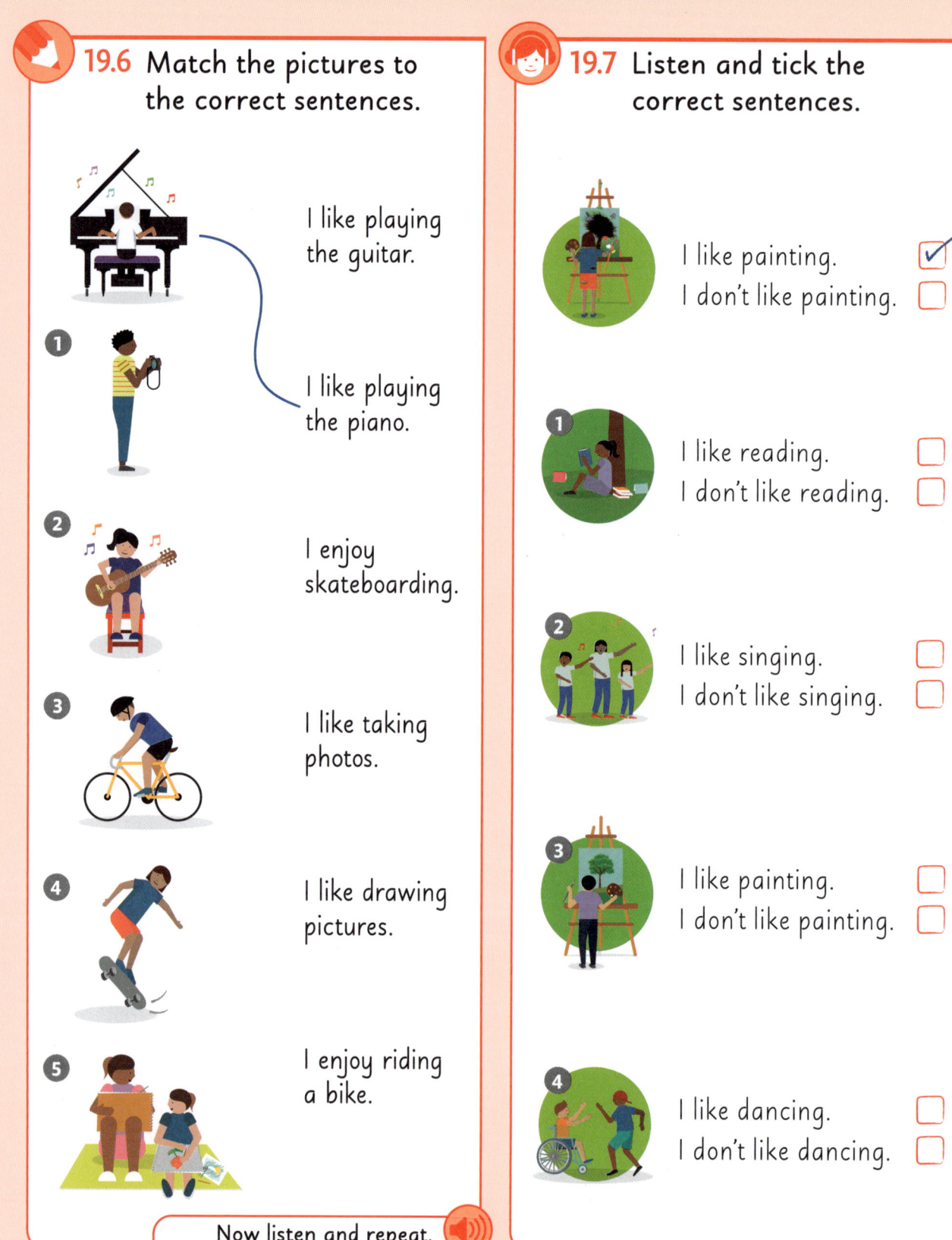

19.6 Match the pictures to the correct sentences.

I like playing the guitar.

I like playing the piano.

1

2

3

I enjoy skateboarding.

I like taking photos.

4

I like drawing pictures.

5

I enjoy riding a bike.

Now listen and repeat.

19.7 Listen and tick the correct sentences.

I like painting. ✓
I don't like painting.

1
I like reading.
I don't like reading.

2
I like singing.
I don't like singing.

3
I like painting.
I don't like painting.

4
I like dancing.
I don't like dancing.

19.8 Look at the pictures and write the correct words in the spaces.

drawing pictures   ~~painting~~   reading
taking photos   riding a bike

I enjoy _painting_ .

1 I like _____ .

2 I like _____ .

3 I enjoy _____ .

4 I like _____ .

Now listen and repeat.

19.9 There are four sentences . Mark the beginning and end of each one and write them below.

Do you like reading? _____

1 _____

2 _____

3 _____

Doyoulikereading?|Yes,Ido.Doyoulikesinging?No,Idon't.

Now listen and repeat.

19.10 Look at the pictures and write the correct words in the spaces.

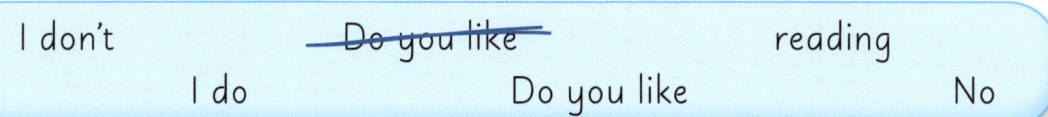

I don't   ~~Do you like~~   reading

I do   Do you like   No

Do you like skateboarding?

Yes, I do.

1 Do you like watching football?

Yes, _____ .

2 Do you like dancing?

No, _____ .

3 _____ playing the piano?

Yes, I do.

4 Do you like singing?

_____ , I don't .

5 Do you like _____ ?

Yes, I do.

Now listen and repeat.

146

19.11 Listen and write the correct answers in the spaces.

~~Yes, I do.~~   No, I don't.
Yes, I do.   No, I don't.
        Yes, I do.

Do you like reading?
Yes, I do.

① Do you like riding a bike?

_____

② Do you like playing the guitar?

_____

③ Do you like singing?

_____

④ Do you like painting?

_____

 19.12 Listen to the song and write the correct words in the spaces.

Have you got hobbies?
Yes, I have.
I ___love___ reading books
and skateboarding, too.

Do you like playing _____ ?
Yes, I do.
I love _____ tennis
and playing _____ , too.

Do you _____ singing?
Yes, I do.
I love _____ songs,
and I love _____ , too.

20 Review: What I like

 **20.1** Listen and read.

I'm Andy. I enjoy playing tennis. I like oranges and pears, but I don't like tomatoes.
I love video games.

My friend Eva enjoys playing table tennis. She likes watermelons, but she doesn't like pears. My friend loves robots.

20.2 Write about the things you and
a friend like then draw a picture.

I'm _____ . I enjoy _____ .
I like _____ and _____ ,
but I don't like _____ .
I love _____ .

My friend _____ enjoys _____ .
_____ likes _____ , but
_____ doesn't like _____ .
My friend loves _____ .

21 Our party clothes

21.1 Listen and write the correct words in the spaces.

1. watch
2. s
3. s
4. s
5. t
6. T-
7. h
8. d
9. h

Happy birthday, Ben!

Thank you, Maria!

trousers   sock   ~~watch~~   shorts

T-shirt   handbag   hat   skirt   dress

jeans   baseball cap   glasses   shoe

jacket   shirt   bag   boot

10 b _____

11 j _____

12 s _____

13 b _____

14 g _____

15 s _____

16 b _____

17 j _____

151

21.2 Look at the pictures and circle the correct words.

shirt / **shorts**

1. glasses / boot

2. T-shirt / hat

3. jacket / shoe

4. trousers / skirt

5. handbag / jeans

Now listen and repeat.

21.3 Look at the pictures and write the correct words in the spaces.

shirt   ~~hat~~   jeans   dress
watch   shorts   jacket

It's a ___hat___ .

1. It's a _____ .

2. It's a _____ .

3. They're _____ .

4. It's a _____ .

5. It's a _____ .

6. They're _____ .

Now listen and repeat.

Listen and tick the correct pictures.

A ☐   B ☑   **1** A ☐   B ☐   **2** A ☐   B ☐

3 A ☐   B ☐   **4** A ☐   B ☐   **5** A ☐   B ☐

21.5 Listen to the song and write the correct words in the spaces.

We're at a ____party____ ,
so let's all _____ and play.
What a fun _____
    for Ben's birthday!

Andy's _____ his
favourite _____ ,
    and Sara's got
a beautiful _____ .

21.6 Look at the pictures and tick the correct sentences.

I'm wearing socks. ☐
I'm wearing glasses. ☑

1

I'm wearing a jacket. ☐
I'm wearing trousers. ☐

2

I'm wearing a hat. ☐
I'm wearing a watch. ☐

3

I'm wearing a watch. ☐
I'm wearing jeans. ☐

4

I'm wearing a dress. ☐
I'm wearing boots. ☐

5

I'm wearing trousers. ☐
I'm wearing a hat. ☐

Now listen and repeat. 🔊

21.7 Listen and match the names to the correct clothes.

Sara   **1** Max   **2** Nick   **3** Kim   **4** James   **5** Maria

jacket

shorts

jeans

baseball cap   shirt   dress

21.8 There are four sentences. Mark the beginning and end of each one and write them below.

Areyouwearingboots? | Yes,Iam.Areyouwearingawatch?No,I'mnot.

Are you wearing boots?

1 _____

2 _____

3 _____

Now listen and repeat.

155

21.9 Look at the pictures and write the correct answers in the spaces.

No, I'm not.   ~~Yes, I am.~~   No, I'm not.   Yes, I am.

Are you wearing my baseball cap?

Yes, I am.

1 Are you wearing my trousers?

2 Are you wearing my shirt?

3 Are you wearing my boots?

Now listen and repeat. 🔊

21.10 Look at the pictures and circle the correct words.

  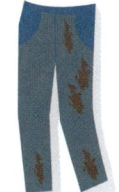

(What a) / What lovely watch!

1 What a / What clean shoes!

2 What a / What dirty jeans!

3 What a / What nice hat!

4 What a / What colourful bag!

5 What a / What nice skirt!

Now listen and repeat.

21.11 Match the pictures to the correct sentences.

 **1**  **2**  **3**  **4**

What lovely trousers!   What a nice watch!   What dirty socks!

What a beautiful dress!   What lovely shorts!

Now listen and repeat.

22 Our day on the beach

22.1 Listen and write the correct words in the spaces.

1 seagull

2 s ___

3 s ___

4 j ___

5 f ___

6 s ___

7 p ___

8 b ___

9 s ___

10 l ___

11 d ___

12 e ___

Maria's eating ice cream.

Sofia's drinking juice.

13) f _____

14) s _____

15) r _____

16) r _____

17) t _____

18) s _____

jellyfish

play football

surf

~~seagull~~

ship

drink juice

eat ice cream

fly a kite

bucket

listen to music

sand

spade

run on the beach

swim in the sea

fish

throw a ball

shell

read a book

22.2 Match the pictures to the correct words.

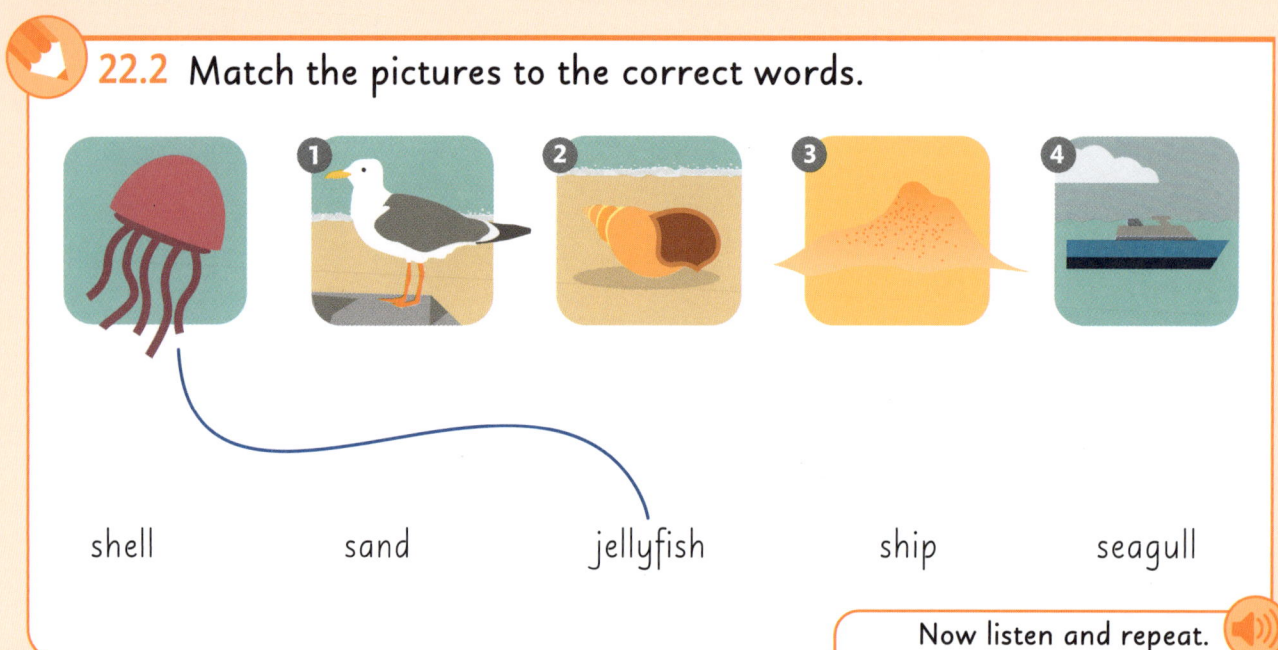

shell   sand   jellyfish   ship   seagull

Now listen and repeat.

22.3 Listen and colour in the pictures.

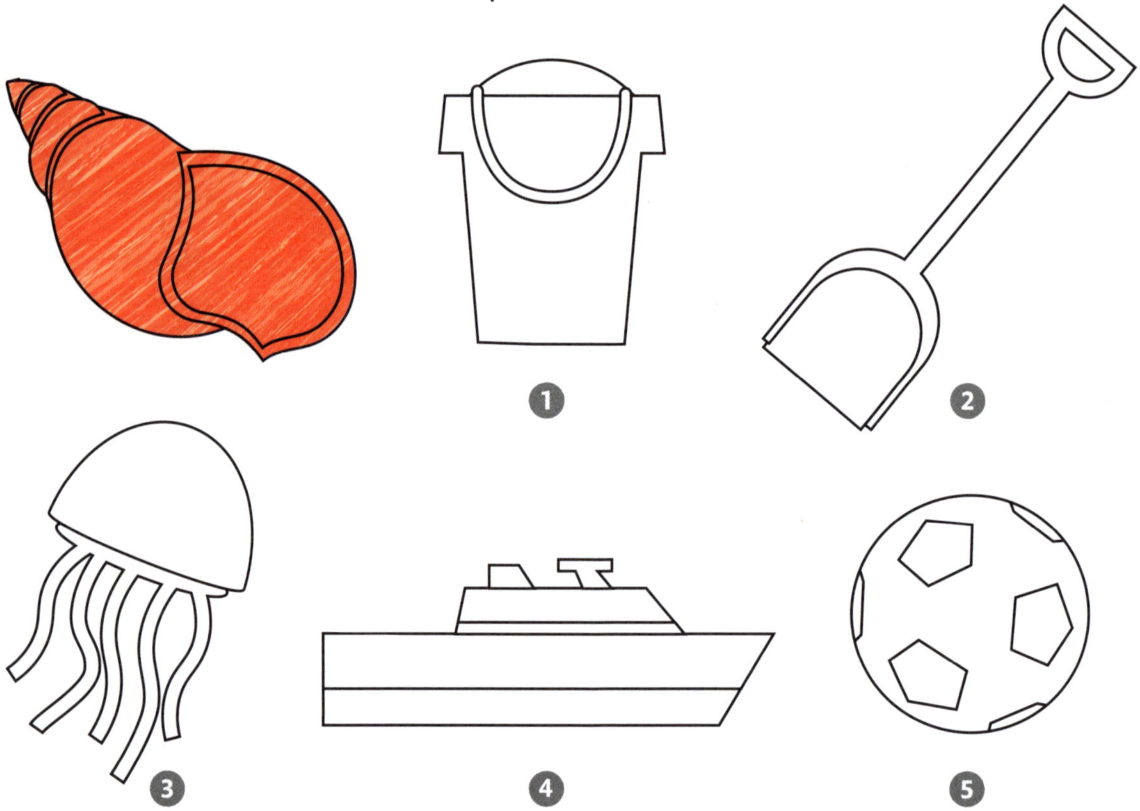

1

2

3

4

5

22.4 Read the sentences and tick the correct pictures.

I'm listening to music.

A ✓   B ☐

1 I'm fishing.

A ☐   B ☐

2 I'm playing football.

A ☐   B ☐

3 I'm reading a book.

A ☐   B ☐

4 I'm throwing a ball.

A ☐   B ☐

5 I'm running on the beach.

A ☐   B ☐

6 I'm surfing.

A ☐   B ☐

7 I'm swimming in the sea.

A ☐   B ☐

Now listen and repeat.

22.5 Look at the pictures and circle the correct words.

(She's) / She isn't reading a book.

❶ He's / He isn't swimming.

❷ He's / He isn't listening to music.

❸ She's / She isn't drinking juice.

❹ She's / She isn't surfing.

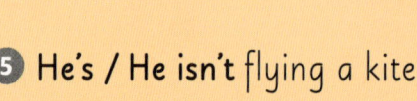

❺ He's / He isn't flying a kite.

❻ She's / She isn't running.

Now listen and repeat.

22.6 Look at the pictures and write the correct words in the spaces.

surfing   ~~throwing~~   playing   listening   drinking   reading

He's ___throwing___ a ball.

❶ She's _____ juice.

❷ She's _____ .

❸ He's _____ football.

❹ She's _____ a book.

❺ He's _____ to music.

Now listen and repeat. 🔊

22.7 Look at the pictures and tick the correct answers.

Is Peter fishing?

Yes, he is. ✓

No, he isn't. ☐

1 Is he reading a book?

Yes, he is. ☐

No, he isn't. ☐

2 Is he flying a kite?

Yes, he is. ☐

No, he isn't. ☐

3 Is she playing football?

Yes, she is. ☐

No, she isn't. ☐

4 Is Maria eating ice cream?

Yes, she is. ☐

No, she isn't. ☐

Now listen and repeat.

Listen and write the correct answers in the spaces.

Yes, she is.   ~~Yes, he is.~~

No, he isn't.   No, she isn't.

Is he playing football?

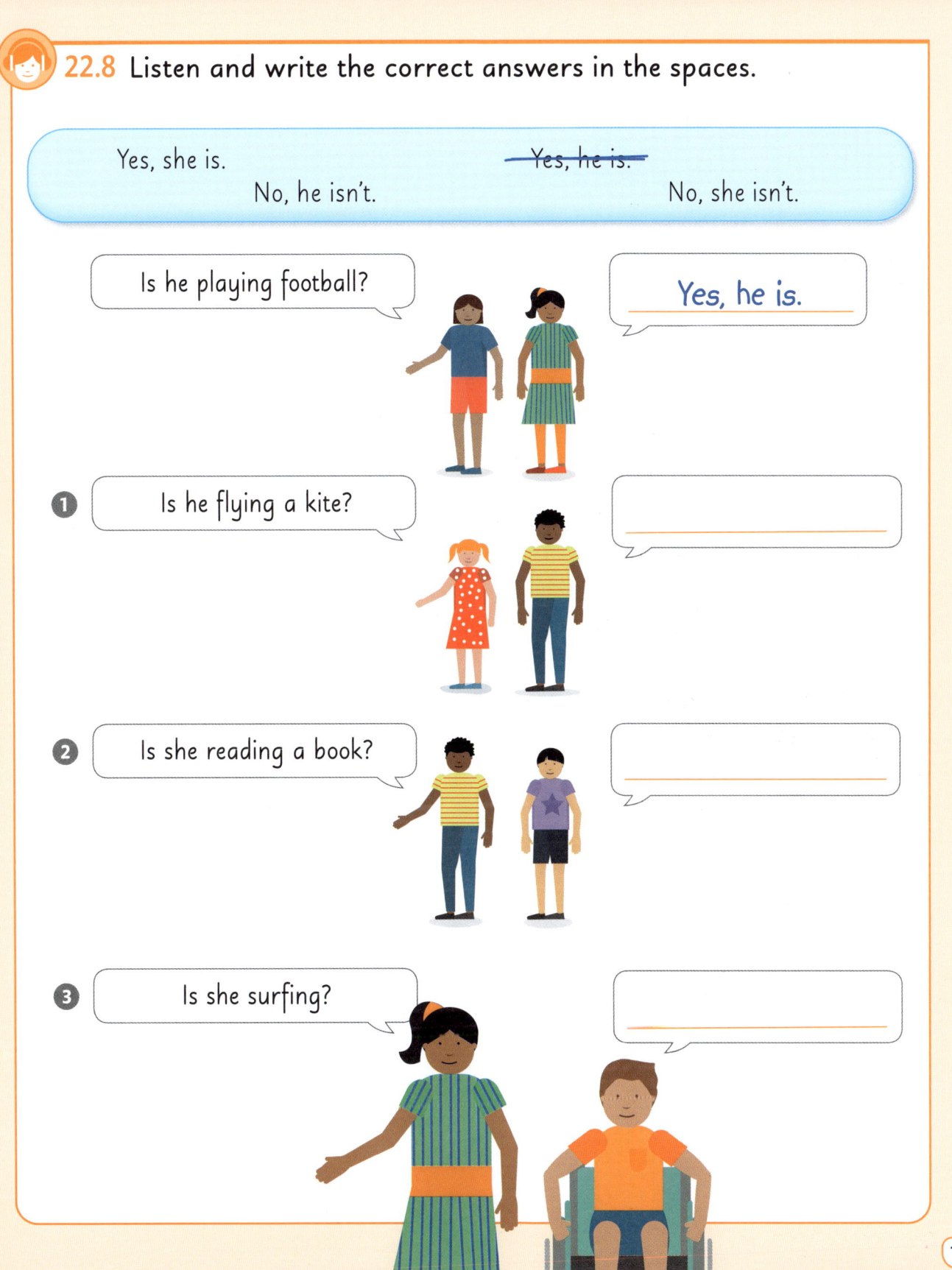

Yes, he is.

1 Is he flying a kite?

2 Is she reading a book?

3 Is she surfing?

23.1 Listen and write the correct words in the spaces.

① pie

② c _____

③ c _____

④ s _____

⑤ b _____

⑥ o _____

⑦ s _____

⑧ r _____

⑨ s _____

Would you like an orange, Andy?

Yes, please.

burger   salad   orange   ~~pie~~

chips   rice   cake   sweets

sausages   drinks   chocolate   juice

noodles   lemonade   water   fruit

10 c _____

12 d _____

11 n _____

16 l _____

15 w _____

13 f _____

14 j _____

23.2 Match the pictures to the correct words.

② ④

① ③

cake   sweets   pie   drinks   fruit

Now listen and repeat.

23.3 Look at the pictures and write the words in the correct place on the crossword.

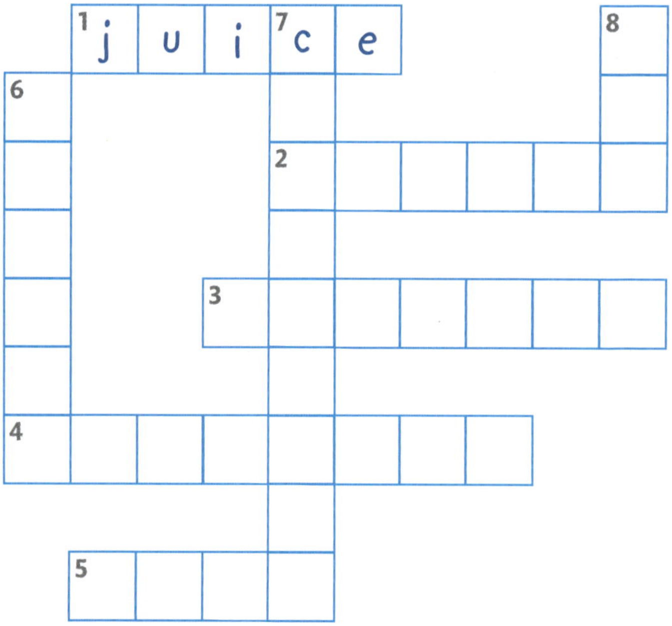

| ¹j | u | i | ⁷c | e | | | ⁸ |

6

2

3

4

5

① ②

③ ④

⑤ ⑥

⑦ ⑧

 **23.4** Listen and match the questions to the correct answers.

What would you like?

I'd like some chips, please.

1 What would you like?

I'd like some water, please.

2 What would you like?

I'd like an orange, please.

3 What would you like?

4 What would you like?

I'd like a burger, please.

I'd like some lemonade, please.

23.5 Look at the pictures and circle the correct words.

I'd like **a** / **some** fruit, please.

❶ I'd like **a** / **some** juice, please.

❷ I'd like **a** / **some** rice, please.

❸ I'd like **an** / **some** orange, please.

❹ I'd like **a** / **some** burger, please.

❺ I'd like **a** / **some** noodles, please.

Now listen and repeat.

23.6 Listen and write the correct words in the spaces.

No, I wouldn't.   No, thank you.   ~~Yes, I would.~~
Yes, please.   Yes, I would.

 Would you like some chocolate?  Yes, I would.

1  Would you like a drink?  _____

2  Would you like some salad?  _____

3  Would you like some chips? 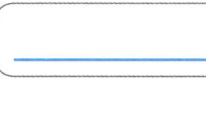 _____

4  Would you like some cake?  _____

23.7 Listen and write the correct words in the spaces.

① ...breakfast...

② m_____

③ e_____   ④ b_____

⑤ l_____

⑥ m_____   ⑦ p_____

⑧ d_____

⑨ r_____

⑩ b_____   ⑪ f_____   ⑫ p_____   ⑬ c_____   ⑭ p_____

egg	lunch	potatoes	~~breakfast~~	bread
pasta	rice		meatball	chicken
beans	fish	milk	dinner	peas

23.8 Listen and match the questions to the correct answers.

What's for breakfast today, Mum?   Meat and potatoes.

❶ What's for lunch today, Dad?   Chicken and peas.

❷ What's for breakfast today, Dad?   Fish and beans.

❸ What's for dinner today, Mum?   Eggs and bread.

❹ What's for lunch today, Mum?   Meatballs and rice.

❺ What's for dinner today, Dad?   Milk and bread.

23.9 There are four sentences. Mark the beginning and end of each one and write them below.

What'sforlunch?/Fishandpotatoes.What'sfordinner?Pastaandmeatballs.

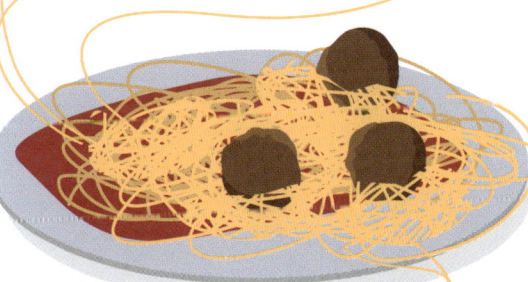

What's for lunch?

❶ _____

❷ _____

❸ _____

Now listen and repeat. 🔊

24 At the park

24.1 Listen and write the correct words in the spaces.

1. boy
2. g
3. b
4. W
5. W

Whose skateboard is this?

It's mine.

baby   woman   girl   ~~boy~~

women   child / kid   person   men

children / kids   man   people

6 p _____

7 p _____

8 c _____

9 c _____

10 m _____

11 m _____

24.2 Listen and tick the correct pictures.

A ☐ B ✓

① A ☐ B ☐

② A ☐ B ☐

③ A ☐ B ☐

24.3 Look at the pictures and write the correct words in the spaces.

girl men ~~baby~~
boy children woman

baby

① _____

② _____

③ _____

④ _____

⑤ _____

Now listen and repeat. 🔊

24.4 Match the pictures to the correct words.

① ② ③ ④

kids   boy   girl   man   baby

Now listen and repeat.

24.5 Read the words and tick the correct pictures.

men

A ☐   B ✓

① person

A ☐   B ☐

② children

A ☐   B ☐

③ man

A ☐   B ☐

④ kid

A ☐   B ☐

⑤ women

A ☐   B ☐

Now listen and repeat.

24.6 Rewrite the questions in the correct order.

bike? | Is | Tom's | this

Is this Tom's bike?

1 Kim's | Is | this | ball?

2 this | Nick's | cat? | Is

3 book? | this | Is | Amy's

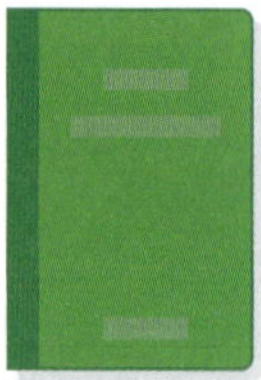

4 Lucy's | Is | this | computer?

5 this | Maria's | jacket? | Is

Now listen and repeat.

24.7 Listen and write the correct names in the spaces.

24.8 Listen again and colour in the pictures.

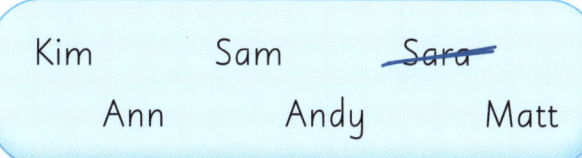
Kim   Sam   ~~Sara~~
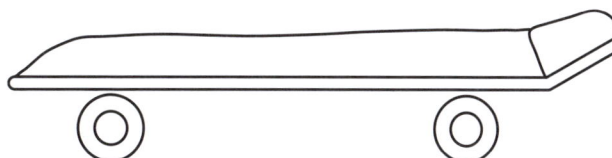
Ann   Andy   Matt

Sara

① _____

   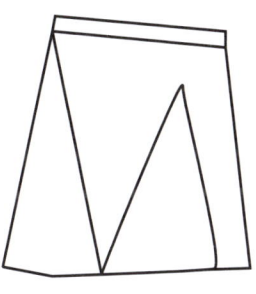   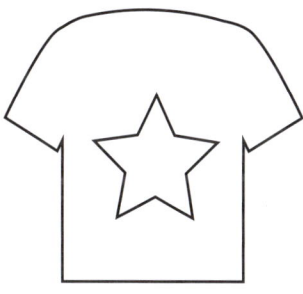

② _____   **③** _____   **④** _____

⑤ _____

24.9 Listen and tick the correct answers.

Whose doll is this?

It's hers. ✓

It's yours. ☐

1 Whose watch is this?

It's mine. ☐

It's his. ☐

2 Whose ruler is this?

It's ours. ☐

It's theirs. ☐

3 Whose apple is this?

It's yours. ☐

It's hers. ☐

4 Whose rabbit is this?

It's mine. ☐

It's theirs. ☐

24.10 Listen and circle the correct words.

Whose bucket is this?

It's (mine) / theirs.

1 Whose camera is this?

It's his / hers.

2 Whose tortoise is this?

It's ours / theirs.

3 Whose handbag is this?

It's hers / mine.

4 Whose juice is this?

It's yours / his.

5 Whose bike is this?

It's mine / theirs.

6 Whose skateboard is this?

It's hers / ours.

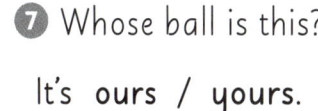

7 Whose ball is this?

It's ours / yours.

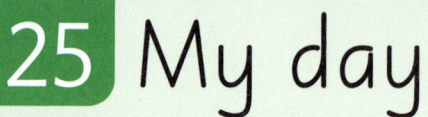

25.1 Listen and write the correct sentences in the spaces.

① I get up.

I eat dinner. I phone my friend.

I go swimming.

~~I get up.~~ I go to sleep.

⑫ I g _____

⑪ I e _____ ⑩ I g _____ ⑨ I p _____

② I m _____

③ I e _____

④ I c _____

I go home.   I make my bed.

I walk to school.   I eat breakfast.

            I clean my teeth.

I eat lunch.   I learn English.

⑤ I w _____

⑧ I g _____   ⑦ I e _____   ⑥ I l _____

25.2 Look at the pictures and tick the correct sentences.

I walk to school. ☐
I eat breakfast. ✓

I go home. ☐
I phone my friend. ☐

I get up. ☐
I make my bed. ☐

I clean my teeth. ☐
I eat dinner. ☐

I go swimming. ☐
I walk to school. ☐

I go to sleep. ☐
I learn English. ☐

Now listen and repeat.

25.3 Rewrite the sentences in the correct order.

bed. | my | make | I

I make my bed.

1. phone | my | I | friend.

2. to | walk | school. | I

3. sleep. | go | I | to

4. my | clean | teeth. | I

5. eat | I | lunch.

Now listen and repeat.

25.4 Look at the clocks and write the correct answers in the spaces.

It's five o'clock. | It's six o'clock. | ~~It's two o'clock.~~
It's nine o'clock. | It's ten o'clock. | It's three o'clock.
It's eleven o'clock. | It's four o'clock. | It's one o'clock.

What time is it?

It's two o'clock.

❶ What time is it?

_____

❷ What time is it?

_____

❸ What time is it?

_____

❹ What time is it?

_____

❺ What time is it?

_____

❻ What time is it?

_____

❼ What time is it?

_____

❽ What time is it?

_____

Now listen and repeat.

25.5 Match the pictures to the correct words.

In the afternoon   At night   In the morning   In the evening

Now listen and repeat.

25.6 Listen and circle the correct words.

I go swimming in the
morning / afternoon.

I walk to school in the
morning / evening.

I eat dinner in the
afternoon / evening.

I go home in the
morning / afternoon.

I go to sleep at
night / afternoon.

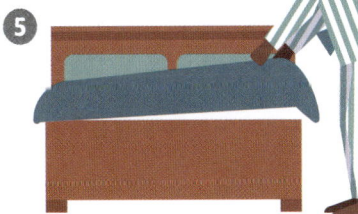

I make my bed in the
evening / morning.

25.7 Read the sentences and write the correct words in the spaces.

in   ~~eight o'clock~~   morning   When do you   at   four o'clock

When do you walk
to school?

I walk to school at
__eight o'clock__ .

1

_____
get up?

I get up at seven o'clock.

2 When do you eat dinner?

I eat dinner _____
the evening.

3 When do you go to sleep?

I go to sleep _____
eight o'clock.

4 When do you go home?

I go home at
_____ .

5 When do you clean
your teeth?

I clean my teeth in the
_____ and at night.

Now listen and repeat.

25.8 Look at the pictures and tick the correct sentences.

He goes to sleep. ✓
He go to sleep. ☐

We walks to school. ☐
We walk to school. ☐

She phones her friend. ☐
She phone her friend. ☐

He cleans his teeth. ☐
He clean his teeth. ☐

They eats dinner. ☐
They eat dinner. ☐

I goes home. ☐
I go home. ☐

Now listen and repeat.

25.9 Write the letters in the correct order.

M d n o a y

<u>M</u> <u>o</u> <u>n</u> <u>d</u> <u>a</u> <u>y</u>

1 T s d u y e a

I _ _ _ _ _ _ _

2 W d n e a s e y d

<u>W</u> _ _ _ _ _ _ _ _ _

3 T u r a s y h d

<u>I</u> _ _ _ _ _ _ _ _

4 F i d y r a

<u>F</u> _ _ _ _ _ _

5 S u t a d y a r

<u>S</u> _ _ _ _ _ _ _ _

6 S d n a y u

<u>S</u> _ _ _ _ _

Now listen and repeat.

25.10 Read the sentences and circle the correct words.

I walk to school (at) / on seven o'clock.

1 I go swimming at / on Tuesdays.

2 I phone my friend at / on Fridays.

3 I eat lunch at / on twelve o'clock.

Now listen and repeat.

25.11 Listen and write the correct answers in the spaces.

I don't.	~~So do I.~~	I don't.	So do I.

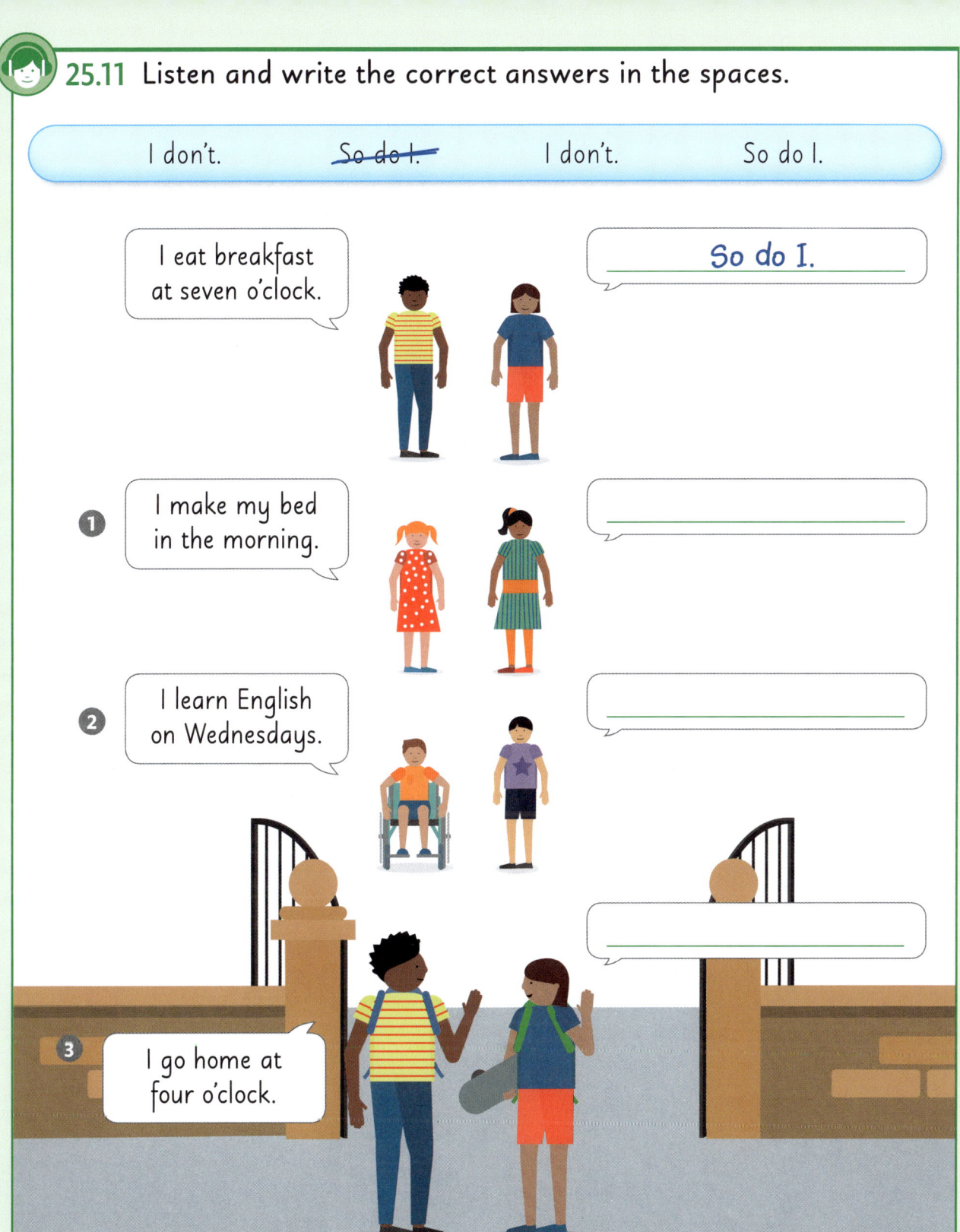

I eat breakfast at seven o'clock.

So do I.

1 I make my bed in the morning.

2 I learn English on Wednesdays.

3 I go home at four o'clock.

26.1 Listen and read.

My name's Maria. Today I'm wearing
a dress and shoes. My favourite food
is cake and I love burgers, too.

I get up at 7 o'clock and I eat breakfast.
In the evening, I phone my friend.
I learn English on Tuesdays.
On Saturdays, I go swimming.

 **26.2** Write about the things you do then draw
a picture of your favourite foods.

My name's _____ . Today I'm wearing
_____ and _____ . My favourite
food is _____ and I love _____ , too.

I get up at _____ and I _____ .
In the evening, I _____ .
I learn English on _____ .
On Saturdays, I _____ .

Handwriting guide

A1 To practise writing English letters, start at the red dot and then follow the arrows.

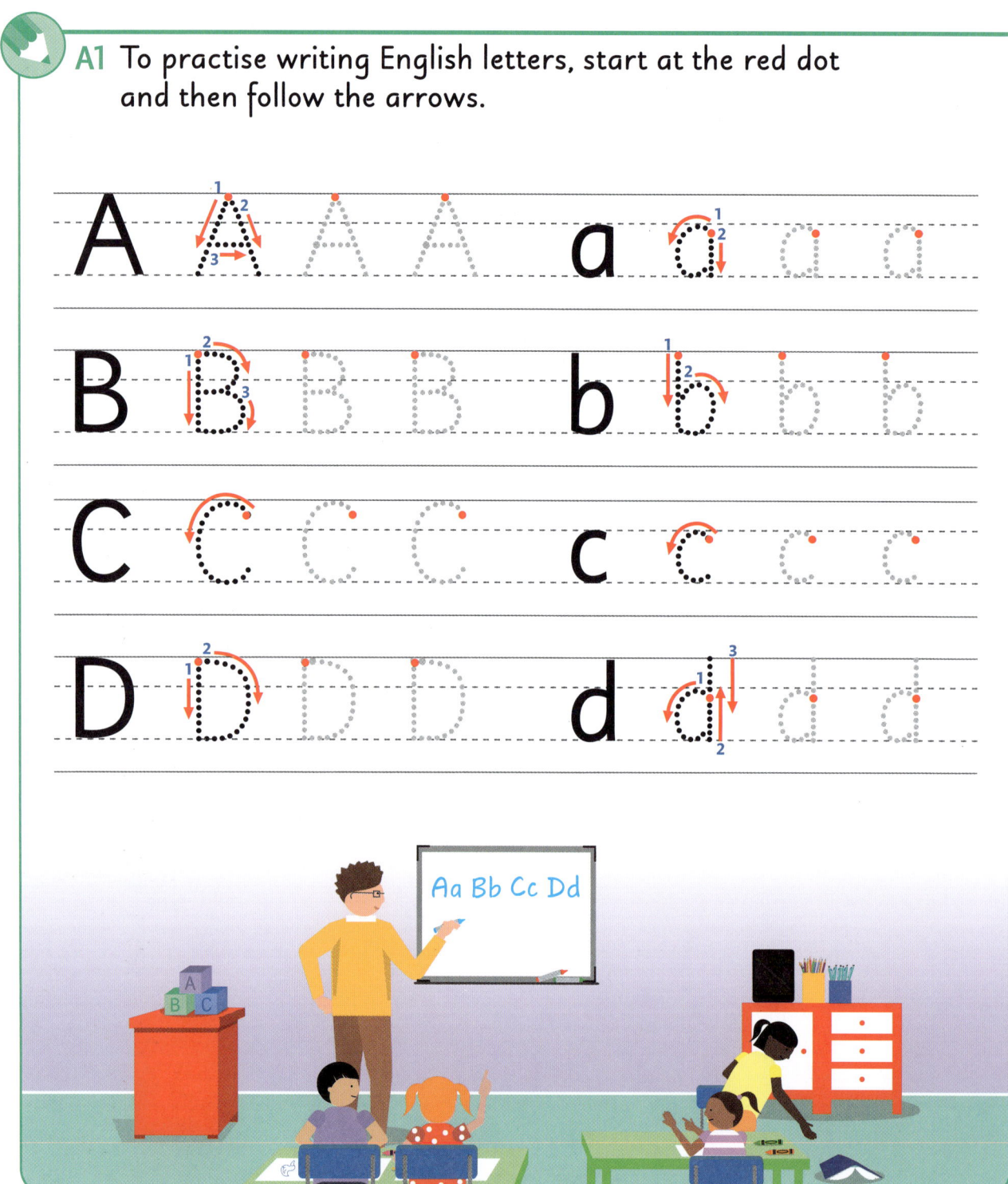

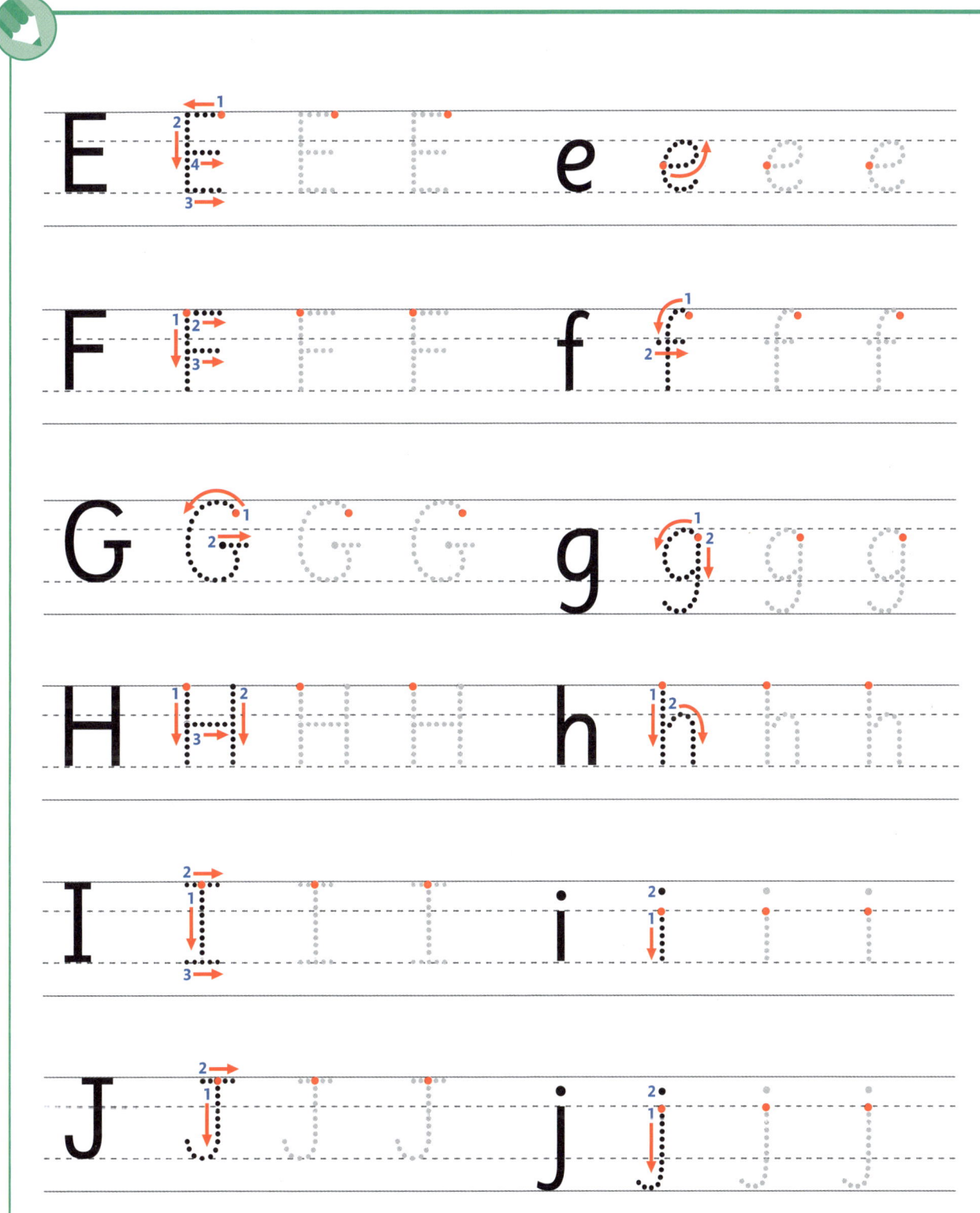

E e

F f

G g

H h

I i

J j

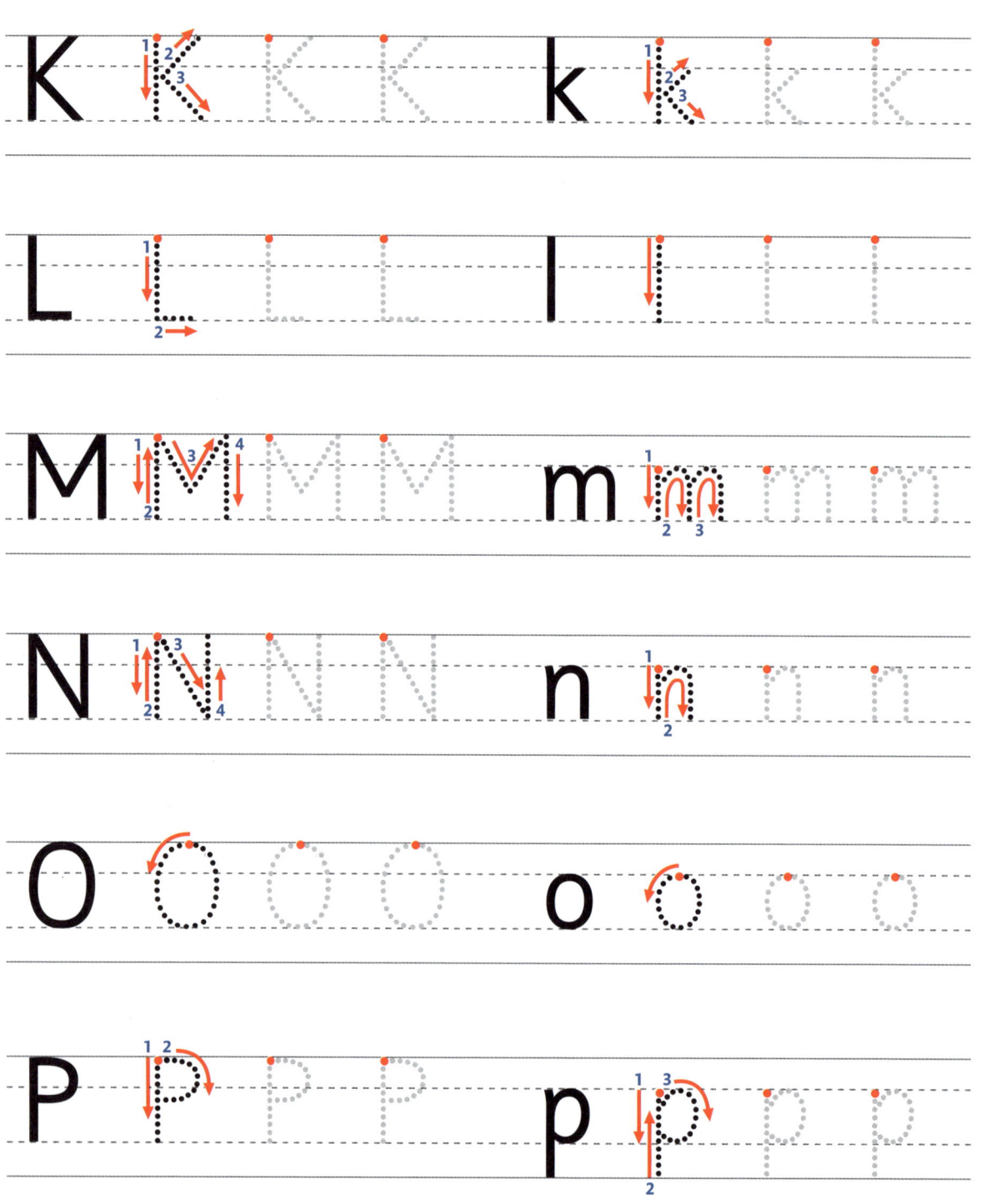

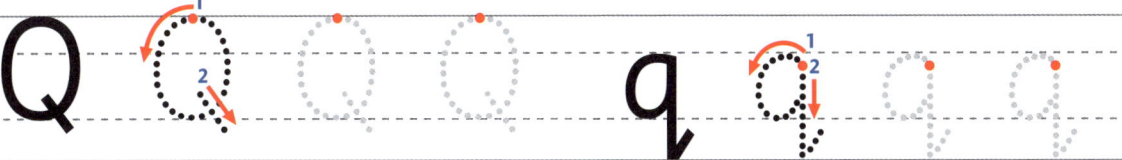

Q Q Q Q q q q q

R R R R r r r r

S S S S s s s s

T T T T t t t t

U U U U u u u u

V V V V v v v v

W w W W W   w w w w w

X x X X X   x x x x x

Y Y Y Y Y   y y y y y

Z Z Z Z Z   z z z z z

Answers

1

1.1

1. Maria
2. Ben
3. Max
4. Andy
5. Sofia
6. Sara

1.2

1. Hi, my **name's** Sara.
2. Hi, I'm **Max**.
3. Hi, **I'm** Andy.
4. Hello, I'm **Maria**.
5. **Hello**, I'm Ben.

1.3

1.3 Find Max and Sara in the picture.

1.4

1. Andy
2. Sara
3. Max
4. Maria
5. Sofia

1.5

1. three
2. seven
3. nine
4. six
5. ten
6. eight
7. five

1.6

1. eight
2. two
3. four
4. one
5. seven

1.7

1. one
2. two
3. five
4. four
5. six

1.8

1. I'm fine, thanks.
2. I'm nine years old.

2

2.1

1. playground
2. numbers
3. letters
4. teacher
5. board
6. classmate
7. alphabet
8. tablet
9. cupboard
10. book

2.2

1. tablet
2. teacher
3. alphabet
4. board

5 playground **6** letters
7 numbers **8** classmate
9 cupboard

2.3
1 cupboard **2** numbers
3 tablet **4** teacher
5 board **6** book

2.4
1 A **2** B **3** A **4** A **5** B

2.5
1 pick up **2** sit down
3 find **4** stand up
5 ask

2.6
1 show **2** listen **3** close
4 find **5** answer

2.7
1 find **2** ask **3** show
4 look **5** open **6** close
7 add **8** answer

2.8
1 **His** name's Andy.
2 **His** name's Ben.
3 **Her** name's Maria.

4 **His** name's Max.
5 **Her** name's Sofia.

2.9
1 His name's Dan.
2 Her name's Bella.
3 His name's Tom.
4 Her name's Anna.
5 Her name's Amy.

2.10
1 Her name's Evie.
2 What's his name?
3 His name's Jack.

3

3.1
1 write **2** read **3** count
4 play **5** spell **6** paint
7 draw

3.2
1 read **2** play **3** write
4 paint

3.3
1 A **2** A **3** B **4** A **5** A

3.4

1. Let's write!
2. Let's count!
3. Let's paint!
4. Let's read!
5. Let's play!

3.5

Hello, **hello**!
What's your **name**?
How are you?
Let's **play** a game.

Let's say hello
to my new friends
Max and Maria,
Sara and **Ben**.

3.6

1. twelve
2. sixteen
3. fifteen
4. twenty

3.7

1. fourteen
2. nineteen
3. eighteen
4. eleven
5. sixteen
6. twenty
7. thirteen
8. fifteen

3.8

1. tablet
2. numbers
3. cars
4. dog
5. cupboard

3.9

1. A
2. B
3. B
4. B

4

4.1

1. pink
2. book
3. crayon
4. rubber
5. pen
6. paper
7. ball
8. notepad
9. purple
10. red
11. bag
12. ruler
13. white
14. brown
15. apple
16. orange
17. green
18. yellow
19. blue
20. pencil
21. grey
22. black
23. watch

4.2

1. crayon
2. rubber
3. pen
4. pencil
5. watch

4.3

1. green
2. pink
3. brown
4. black
5. grey

4.4

1. purple
2. bag
3. white
4. notepad
5. orange
6. yellow
7. paper

4.5

1. A
2. A
3. A
4. B
5. B

4.6

1. It's a watch.
2. It's a ball.
3. They're rulers.

4.7

1. What are **these**?
2. It's an **apple**.
3. **It's** a pencil.
4. **What are** these?
5. **They're** notepads.

4.8

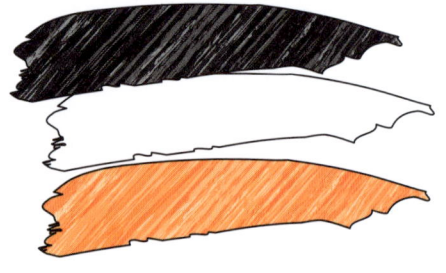

4.9

1. B   2. A   3. B   4. A

4.10

1. It's purple.
2. It's red.
3. It's orange.

5

5.1

1. zebra
2. giraffe
3. lion
4. elephant
5. hippo
6. parrot
7. tiger
8. monkey

9 bear
11 snake
13 bird
15 penguin
17 lizard

10 frog
12 polar bear
14 whale
16 crocodile

5.2

1 hippo
3 tiger
5 crocodile

2 parrot
4 elephant

5.3

5.4

1 whale
3 zebra

2 lion
4 bear

5.5

Animals, animals
everywhere!
a **lion**, a giraffe,
and a **polar bear**.

A **whale** and
a **penguin**,
a tiger and a **snake**,
animals, animals,
they are great!

5.6

1 What's **that?** 2 **They're** hippos.
3 **What's** that?

5.7

1 It's a zebra. 2 It's a crocodile.
3 They're parrots.

5.8

1 It's a lizard.
2 They're penguins.
3 It's a parrot.
4 They're elephants.
5 It's a bird.

5.9

1 They're tigers. 2 What's that?
3 It's an elephant.

5.10
1 A **2** A **3** B **4** B **5** A

5.11
1 My favourite animal is a **lizard**.
2 My favourite animal is a **bear**.
3 My favourite animal is a **bird**.
4 My favourite animal is an **elephant**.
5 My favourite animal is a **monkey**.

6

6.1
1 my family
2 my grandmother / grandma
3 my grandfather / grandpa
4 my father / dad
5 my mother / mum
6 my brother
7 my sister
8 me
9 my uncle
10 my aunt
11 my cousin

6.2
1 my grandma **2** my cousin
3 my family **4** my uncle
5 my grandpa

6.3
1 brother **2** mother
3 grandfather **4** sister

6.4
1 She's my **cousin**.
2 He's my **uncle**.
3 She's my **sister**.
4 He's my **dad**.
5 She's my **grandma**.

6.5
1 No, he isn't. **2** No, she isn't.
3 Yes, she is.

6.6
1 doctor **2** teacher
3 chef **4** firefighter

6.7

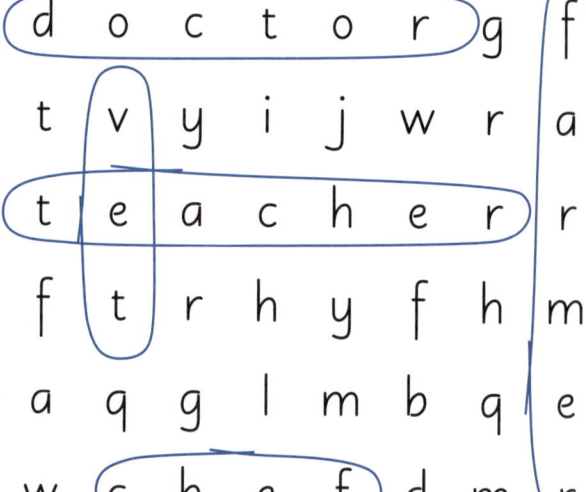

6.8

1. She's a **doctor**.
2. He's a **teacher**.
3. She's a **chef**.
4. She's a **police officer**.

6.9

1. She's a doctor.
2. She's a chef.
3. He's a farmer.
4. She's a teacher.
5. She's a police officer.

6.10

Who's this?
She's my **mother**.
Who's that?
He's my **brother**.

My **dad** is a teacher,
my **mum** is a vet,
Grandpa's a **doctor**,
And Grandma's a **chef**!

7

7.1

1. poster
2. computer
3. mouse
4. keyboard

5. lamp
6. toy box
7. desk
8. doll
9. chair
10. car
11. camera
12. rug
13. bed
14. teddy bear
15. baseball bat
16. ball
17. skateboard
18. tennis racket

7.2

1. skateboard
2. chair
3. toy box
4. car
5. lamp

7.3

1. A
2. B
3. B
4. A

7.4

1. B
2. A
3. B
4. B
5. A

7.5

1. doll
2. skateboard
3. toy box
4. computer

7.6

1. **That's** my ball.
2. **These are** my cameras.
3. **Those are** my teddy bears.
4. **That's** my toy box.
5. **This is** my tennis racket.

7.7

1 Andy
2 Andy
3 Andy
4 Maria
5 Maria
6 Andy
7 Maria

7.8

1 No, I haven't.
2 Yes, I have.
3 Yes, I have.
4 No, I haven't.

7.9

1 No, I haven't.
2 Yes, I have.
3 No, I haven't.
4 Yes, I have.
5 No, I haven't.

7.10

This is my **toy box**
and these are my **toys**,
I've got a **ball**
and a **skateboard**, too.
Toys are fantastic!
Toys are cool!

9

9.1

1 tired
2 hungry
3 thirsty
4 scared
5 hot
6 cold
7 excited
8 sad
9 happy

9.2

1 cold
2 scared
3 hungry
4 sad
5 hot

9.3

1 A
2 A
3 B
4 B
5 A

9.4

1 thirsty
2 tired
3 happy
4 excited

9.5

Are you **happy**?
Yes, we are!
We are at the fair.

Are you **tired**?
No, we aren't.
We aren't tired
or **scared**!

9.6

1 We're happy.
2 We're thirsty.
3 We're really hot.

9.7

1 We're happy.
2 They're cold.
3 They're hot.
4 We're sad.
5 They're thirsty.
6 They're tired.
7 We're scared.

9.8

1 We're really **excited**.
2 They're **hot**.
3 We're **happy**.
4 We're **really** tired.

9.9

1 Yes, we are.
2 Yes, we are.
3 No, they're not.
4 No, we're not.
5 Yes, they are.

9.10

1 Yes, they are.
2 Yes, we are.

3 No, we're not.
4 No, they're not.

9.11

1 No, they're not.
2 No, we're not.
3 Yes, they are.
4 No, they're not.
5 No, we're not.
6 Yes, we are.
7 Yes, they are.

10

10.1

1 rabbit
2 tortoise
3 dog
4 mouse
5 collar
6 spider
7 cat
8 vet
9 fish

10.2

1 old
2 nice
3 scary
4 dirty
5 clean
6 beautiful
7 big
8 small

10.3

1. rabbit
2. fish
3. spider
4. collar

10.4

1. cat
2. vet
3. mouse
4. dog
5. tortoise

10.5

1. A
2. A
3. B
4. B

10.6

I've got a **cat**,
she's **black** and **small**.
She likes to run
and play with a ball.

Maria's got a **tortoise**,
his name is Socks.
He's **old** and **green**
and he's in this box.

10.7

1. Sara's got a tortoise.
2. Ben's got a rabbit.
3. She's got a fish.
4. She's got a cat.
5. He's got a cat.

10.8

1. B
2. B
3. B
4. A
5. B

10.9

1. Yes, he has.
2. Yes, she has.
3. No, he hasn't.

10.10

1. A
2. A
3. B
4. A
5. B

10.11

1. The mouse.
2. Which one is scary?
3. The spider!

11

11.1

1. hair
2. nose
3. face
4. long hair
5. mouth
6. body
7. hand
8. arm
9. fingers
10. leg
11. toes
12. foot
13. feet
14. head
15. short hair
16. eye
17. ear
18. teeth

11.2

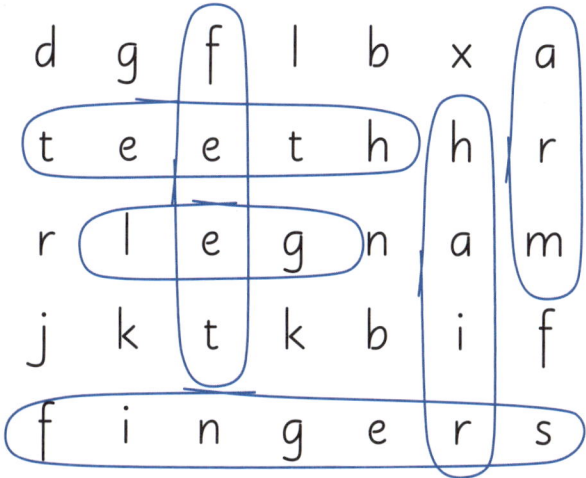

d g **f** l b x **a**
t e e t h h **r**
r **l e g** n a **m**
j k **t** k b i f
f i n g e r s

11.3

1. long hair
2. ear
3. teeth
4. body

11.4

1. mouth
2. nose
3. head
4. foot
5. hand

11.5

1. A
2. B
3. B

11.6

1. The robot's got **purple** eyes.
2. It's got red **teeth**.
3. It's got purple **legs**.
4. The robot's got **blue** feet.
5. It's got a **yellow** nose.
6. The robot's got orange **hands**.

11.7

11.8

1. Yes, it has.
2. No, it hasn't.
3. No, it hasn't.
4. Yes, it has.
5. No, it hasn't.

11.9

1. No, it hasn't.
2. Yes, it has.
3. No, it hasn't.
4. Yes, it has.
5. Yes, it has.

11.10

1. clap
2. touch
3. move
4. point

11.11

Clap your hands,
touch your nose,
move your feet,
point your toes!

Point one **finger**,
move your head,
wave your arms,
touch one leg!

12

12.1

1 airport
2 aeroplane
3 street
4 train
5 bike
6 zoo
7 park
8 bookshop
9 lake
10 boat
11 helicopter
12 school
13 fire station
14 block of flats
15 hospital
16 house
17 shop
18 lorry
19 car
20 bus
21 motorbike

12.2

1 bus
2 school
3 bike
4 hospital
5 lorry

12.3

1 A   2 B   3 A   4 B   5 A

12.4

1 car
2 train
3 lake
4 park

12.5

This is my town,
there's a **park**
and a **zoo**.
There's an **airport**,
a **lake**, and
a fire station, too.

This is my town,
there are **cars** and
a **school**.
This is my town,
I love it, it's cool.

12.6

1 **There are** two shops.
2 **There's** a fire station.
3 **There's** a zoo.
4 **There are** three houses.
5 **There are** four cars.

12.7

1 A   2 B   3 B   4 A   5 A

12.8

1 in front of 2 between
3 next to

12.9

1 It's **behind** the green car.
2 It's **in front of** the lake.
3 It's **next to** the school.
4 It's **between** the hospital
and the bookshop.
5 It's **in front of** the hospital.

12.10

1 It's behind the school.
2 It's between the airport
and the block of flats.
3 It's next to the lake.
4 It's behind the hospital.
5 It's between the fire station
and the shop.

13

13.1

1 garden 2 bedroom
3 clock 4 plants
5 wall 6 window
7 floor 8 armchair
9 bookcase 10 bathroom

11 mirror 12 bath
13 living room 14 television/TV
15 sofa 16 hall
17 door 18 mat
19 lights 20 kitchen
21 fridge 22 dining room
23 flowers 24 table
25 chair

13.2

1 dining room 2 living room
3 kitchen 4 bedroom
5 hall

13.3

1 armchair 2 window
3 table 4 lights

13.4

1 sofa 2 door
3 fridge

13.5

1 clock
2 bookcase
3 chair
4 plants

13.6

1 on 2 under

13.7

1. The cat is **in** the bath.
2. The plants are **under** the window.
3. The cat is **on** the mat.
4. The bookcase is **under** the lights.
5. The flowers are **on** the table.

13.8

1. A 2. B 3. A 4. A

13.9

The TV's **in**
the living room,
the **mat** is in the **hall**.

Where's the **clock**?
It's **on** my
bedroom **wall**.

13.10

1. No, there isn't.
2. Yes, there is.
3. No, there isn't.
4. Yes, there is.
5. **Is there** a table in the dining room?

13.11

1. No, there aren't.
2. No, there aren't.
3. Yes, there are.
4. Yes, there are.
5. No, there aren't.

15

15.1

1. pig
2. tractor
3. tree
4. sheep
5. barn
6. pond
7. duck
8. chicken
9. cow
10. the sun
11. field
12. goat
13. donkey
14. bee
15. tail
16. horse

15.2

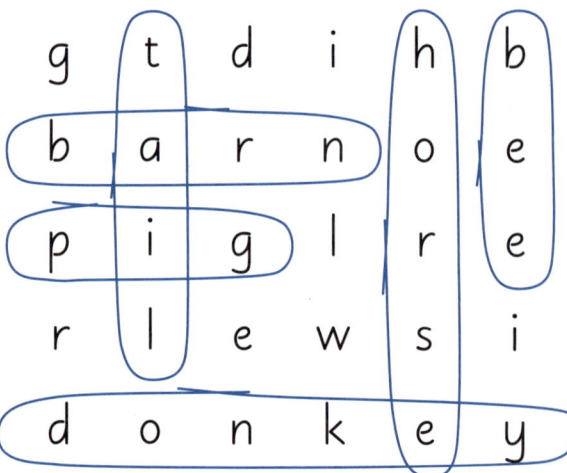

15.3

1. B 2. A 3. B 4. A 5. B

15.4
1 pond 2 tractor 3 the sun
4 tail 5 tree

15.5
1 field
2 barn
3 donkey
4 sheep
5 goat

15.6
1 There are five.
2 There are four.
3 There are three.
4 There are seven.
5 There are six.
6 There are two.

15.7
1 **There are** three.
2 **There's** one.
3 **There are** four.
4 **There's** one.

15.8
1 It's **behind** the tree.
2 It's **next to** the pond.
3 They're **in front of** the barn.

15.9
Where are the **ducks**?
They're on the **pond**!

Where are the **goats**?
They're **in** the field!

Where are the **cows**?
They're in the **barn**!

Where are the animals?
They're **on** my farm!

15.10
1 The ducks are on the pond.
2 The sheep are in front of the barn.
3 The horse is under the tree.

16

16.1
1 basketball 2 baseball
3 football 4 tennis
5 badminton 6 swimming
7 table tennis 8 ice hockey

16.2
1 badminton 2 tennis
3 swimming

16.3

1 B **2** A **3** B **4** B **5** B

16.4

1 jump **2** swim
3 play tennis **4** play ice hockey
5 catch **6** bounce
7 kick **8** throw
9 hit

16.5

1 swim **2** kick
3 catch **4** hit

16.6

1 A **2** A **3** B **4** B **5** B

16.7

1 throw
2 jump
3 bounce
4 catch

16.8

1 play badminton
2 play football
3 play baseball
4 play basketball
5 play ice hockey

16.9

1 I **can** play tennis.
2 I **can't** play baseball.
3 I **can't** play ice hockey.
4 I **can** play basketball.
5 I **can't** play badminton.
6 I **can** play football.

16.10

1 No, I can't.
2 No, I can't.
3 Yes, I can.
4 Yes, I can.

16.11

1 Yes, **he can.**
2 **Can she** run?
3 No, **she can't.**
4 Yes, **she can.**
5 **Can he** play baseball?

16.12

1 Yes, she can.
2 No, she can't.
3 Yes, he can.

16.13

1 Yes, she can.
2 Can he swim?
3 No, he can't.

17

17.1
1. grapes
2. lemons
3. bananas
4. limes
5. kiwis
6. mangoes
7. pineapples
8. tomatoes
9. onions
10. apples
11. pears
12. oranges
13. watermelons
14. coconuts
15. carrots
16. potatoes
17. meat
18. fish
19. fruit
20. vegetables

17.2
1. kiwis
2. pears
3. apples
4. fruit
5. grapes
6. limes
7. meat
8. lemons

17.3
1. watermelons
2. carrots
3. vegetables
4. coconuts

17.4
Apples and oranges,
pears and mangoes, too.
Here are nice potatoes,
and meat and fish for you.

17.5

17.6
1. I like tomatoes **and** carrots.
2. I don't like potatoes **or** onions.
3. I **like** lemons and limes.
4. I don't like apples **or** coconuts.
5. I like mangoes **and** watermelons.

17.7
1. Yes, I do.
2. No, I don't.
3. No, I don't.
4. Yes, I do.

17.8

1. Can I have **some** onions, please?
2. Can I have **a** lemon, please?
3. Can I have **some** pears, please?
4. Can I have **an** orange, please?
5. Can I have **some** carrots, please?

17.9

1. A 2. B 3. A 4. A 5. B

18

18.1

1. alien
2. puppet
3. teddy bear
4. action figure
5. ball
6. doll
7. monster
8. car
9. rocket
10. the moon
11. stars
12. robot
13. balloons
14. train
15. video game
16. board game

18.2

1. A 2. B 3. B

18.3

1. doll 2. ball 3. train
4. stars

18.4

1. teddy bear
2. the moon
3. board game
4. puppet

18.5

1. monster
2. car
3. robot

18.6

1. No, she doesn't.
2. Yes, she does.
3. No, he doesn't.

18.7

1. She **doesn't like** puppets.
2. Maria **likes** aliens.
3. He **doesn't like** cars.
4. Sara **likes** rockets.
5. Max **likes** monsters.
6. He **doesn't like** dolls.
7. She **likes** balloons.

18.8

1. I don't.
2. Me too!
3. I don't.

18.9

Maria likes **dolls**,
but she doesn't like **puppets**.
Andy likes **cars**,
but he doesn't like **rockets**.
I like **trains** and video games,
and my favourite toy
is my **monster**!

18.10

19

19.1

1 ride a bike
2 watch football
3 skateboard
4 draw pictures
5 paint
6 read
7 sing
8 dance
9 play the guitar
10 play the piano
11 take photos

19.2

1 B 2 B 3 A 4 A 5 A

19.3

1 skateboard
2 play the piano
3 sing
4 watch football

19.4

1 play the guitar
2 take photos
3 ride a bike
4 play the piano

19.5

1 paint 2 read
3 sing

19.6

1 I like taking photos.
2 I like playing the guitar.
3 I enjoy riding a bike.
4 I enjoy skateboarding.
5 I like drawing pictures.

19.7

1. I like reading.
2. I don't like singing.
3. I don't like painting.
4. I like dancing.

19.8

1. I like **drawing pictures**.
2. I like **riding a bike**.
3. I enjoy **taking photos**.
4. I like **reading**.

19.9

1. Yes, I do.
2. Do you like singing?
3. No, I don't.

19.10

1. Yes, **I do**.
2. No, **I don't**.
3. **Do you like** playing the piano?
4. **No**, I don't.
5. Do you like **reading**?

19.11

1. No, I don't.
2. No, I don't.
3. Yes, I do.
4. Yes, I do.

19.12

Have you got hobbies?
Yes, I have.
I **love** reading books
and skateboarding, too.

Do you like playing **tennis**?
Yes, I do.
I love **playing** tennis
and playing **football**, too.

Do you **enjoy** singing?
Yes, I do.
I love **singing** songs,
and I love **dancing**, too.

21

21.1

1. watch
2. sock
3. skirt
4. shorts
5. trousers
6. T-shirt
7. hat
8. dress
9. handbag
10. baseball cap
11. jeans
12. shoe
13. boot
14. glasses
15. shirt
16. bag
17. jacket

21.2
1 glasses 2 T-shirt 3 shoe
4 skirt   5 handbag

21.3
1 It's a **watch**.   2 It's a **shirt**.
3 They're **jeans**. 4 It's a **dress**.
5 It's a **jacket**.   6 They're **shorts**.

21.4
1 A   2 B   3 A   4 B   5 A

21.5
We're at a **party**,
so let's all **dance** and play.
What a fun **party**
for Ben's birthday!

Andy's **wearing** his
favourite **T-shirt**,
and Sara's got
a beautiful **skirt**.

21.6
1 I'm wearing a jacket.
2 I'm wearing a hat.
3 I'm wearing a watch.
4 I'm wearing boots.
5 I'm wearing trousers.

21.7
1 shirt
2 baseball cap
3 jeans
4 shorts
5 dress

21.8
1 Yes, I am.
2 Are you wearing a watch?
3 No, I'm not.

21.9
1 No, I'm not.
2 No, I'm not.
3 Yes, I am.

21.10
1 **What** clean shoes!
2 **What** dirty jeans!
3 **What a** nice hat!
4 **What a** colourful bag!
5 **What a** nice skirt!

21.11
1 What dirty socks!
2 What lovely trousers!
3 What lovely shorts!
4 What a beautiful dress!

22

22.1
1. seagull
2. ship
3. surf
4. jellyfish
5. fly a kite
6. sand
7. play football
8. bucket
9. spade
10. listen to music
11. drink juice
12. eat ice cream
13. fish
14. swim in the sea
15. run on the beach
16. read a book
17. throw a ball
18. shell

22.2
1. seagull
2. shell
3. sand
4. ship

22.3

22.4
1. A   2. B   3. B
4. B   5. A   6. B   7. B

22.5
1. **He isn't** swimming.
2. **He's** listening to music.
3. **She isn't** drinking juice.
4. **She isn't** surfing.
5. **He's** flying a kite.
6. **She's** running.

22.6
1. She's **drinking** juice.
2. She's **surfing**.

3 He's **playing** football.

4 She's **reading** a book.

5 He's **listening** to music.

22.7

1 No, he isn't.

2 Yes, he is.

3 No, she isn't.

4 Yes, she is.

22.8

1 No, he isn't.   2 No, she isn't.

3 Yes, she is.

23

23.1

1 pie   2 cake

3 chips   4 sweets

5 burger   6 orange

7 salad   8 rice

9 sausages   10 chocolate

11 noodles   12 drinks

13 fruit   14 juice

15 water   16 lemonade

23.2

1 fruit   2 drinks

3 cake   4 sweets

23.3

1 juice   2 orange

3 noodles   4 sausages

5 rice   6 drinks

7 chocolate   8 pie

23.4

1 I'd like some chips, please.

2 I'd like some lemonade, please.

3 I'd like a burger, please.

4 I'd like some water, please.

23.5

1 I'd like **some** juice, please.

2 I'd like **some** rice, please.

3 I'd like **an** orange, please.

4 I'd like **a** burger, please.

5 I'd like **some** noodles, please.

23.6

1 No, thank you.

2 Yes, please.

3 Yes, I would.

4 No, I wouldn't.

23.7

1 breakfast   2 milk

3 egg   4 bread

5 lunch   6 meatball

7 pasta

8 dinner

9 rice

10 beans

11 fish

12 potatoes

13 chicken

14 peas

23.8

1 Fish and beans.

2 Milk and bread.

3 Meat and potatoes.

4 Chicken and peas.

5 Meatballs and rice.

23.9

1 Fish and potatoes.

2 What's for dinner?

3 Pasta and meatballs.

24

24.1

1 boy

2 girl

3 baby

4 woman

5 women

6 person

7 people

8 child / kid

9 children / kids

10 man

11 men

24.2

1 A   **2** A   **3** B

24.3

1 children

2 men

3 girl

4 woman

5 boy

24.4

1 man

2 kids

3 baby

4 boy

24.5

1 A   **2** B   **3** A   **4** A   **5** B

24.6

1 Is this Kim's ball?

2 Is this Nick's cat?

3 Is this Amy's book?

4 Is this Lucy's computer?

5 Is this Maria's jacket?

24.7

1 Ann

2 Matt

3 Kim

4 Sam

5 Andy

24.8

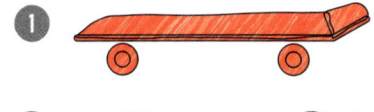

24.9

1 It's his. 2 It's ours. 3 It's yours.
4 It's theirs.

24.10

1 It's **his**.   2 It's **ours**.
3 It's **mine**.   4 It's **yours**.
5 It's **theirs**. 6 It's **hers**.
7 It's **ours**.

25

25.1

1 I get up.
2 I make my bed.
3 I eat breakfast.
4 I clean my teeth.
5 I walk to school.

6 I learn English.
7 I eat lunch.
8 I go home.
9 I phone my friend.
10 I go swimming.
11 I eat dinner.
12 I go to sleep.

25.2

1 I go home.   2 I get up.
3 I eat dinner.   4 I go swimming.
5 I learn English.

25.3

1 I phone my friend.
2 I walk to school.
3 I go to sleep.
4 I clean my teeth.
5 I eat lunch.

25.4

1 It's ten o'clock.
2 It's five o'clock.
3 It's one o'clock.
4 It's six o'clock.
5 It's four o'clock.
6 It's nine o'clock.
7 It's three o'clock.
8 It's eleven o'clock.

25.5

1 In the afternoon
2 In the evening　　3 At night

25.6

1 I walk to school in the **morning**.
2 I eat dinner in the **evening**.
3 I go home in the **afternoon**.
4 I go to sleep at **night**.
5 I make my bed in the **morning**.

25.7

1 **When do you** get up?
2 I eat dinner **in** the evening.
3 I go to sleep **at** eight o'clock.
4 I go home at **four o'clock**.
5 I clean my teeth in the **morning** and at night.

25.8

1 We walk to school.
2 She phones her friend.
3 He cleans his teeth.
4 They eat dinner.
5 I go home.

25.9

1 Tuesday　　2 Wednesday
3 Thursday　　4 Friday
5 Saturday　　6 Sunday

25.10

1 I go swimming **on** Tuesdays.
2 I phone my friend **on** Fridays.
3 I eat lunch **at** twelve o'clock.

25.11

1 I don't.　　2 I don't.　　3 So do I.

Acknowledgments

The publisher would like to thank:

Ankita Awasthi Tröger for administrative assistance; Elizabeth Blakemore for editorial assistance; Laura Gardner for design assistance; Christine Stroyan for proofreading and audio script management and recording; and ID Audio for audio recording and production.

All images © Dorling Kindersley Limited